INTRODUCTION

Nothing is more mysterious than the sea, nor as treacherous. In her fathomless depths, she holds a multitude of secrets, which she occasionally reveals, sparingly and reluctantly. Her sunken carpet is strewn with old relics, once wondrous vessels that disappeared from the surface of the sea, often without leaving trace as to where or why they vanished. With them perished the souls of those who left behind unfinished desires and dreams and the embrace of cherished loved ones. Even today, we hear the names of those so recently departed, and beside the names we read "Lost at Sea." Do their restless spirits, one wonders, still ride the swirling currents and rolling waves, and is it their voices we hear crying out in the shrieking winds of gales and hurricanes?

No matter how ingenious the ship designer, it seems, nor how skilled the mariner, the cruel Atlantic unfailingly makes claim on her tithe of men and ships each year. She is all the more challenged to wrestle and subdue the ones we like to call "unsinkable." Which was more seaworthy, one may ask, the MAYFLOWER of 1620, or the twentieth century TITANIC? They are all the same to the brooding, often boisterous Atlantic. She has always been the most temperamental of the seven sisters, constantly testing wooden ships and challenging iron men. Those who woo her will testify that she changes moods in the flicker of a helmsman's lash, from tranquil calm to frothing tempest. As any old salt will tell you, she is unpredictable and often full of fury, but in her wrath she provides many bizarre, often macabre sagas of man's will to survive.

These are terrible tales, filled with intrigue and suspense, and all true. Perhaps the vessels mentioned here are not haunted ships, but merely victims of unusual circumstance or coincidence. Possibly these are but illusions of superstitious seamen, but in each case, the Atlantic Ocean has prompted the events that are recorded on these pages, and only she can provide the answers to these mysteries.

Bob Cahill

Mike Purcell stands at the second floor entrance to the Miller's Wharf haunted shack in Salem, Massachusetts.

The barge GLENDOWER sits at wharfside after her crew found their captain hacked to death by an axe in his cabin.

I
THE BARGE AT MILLER'S WHARF

It was usually just before Halloween that I'd hear from Mike Purcell about giving a ghost talk at his popular Salem restaurant. Salem, known throughout America as "the Witch City", is crowded with tourists at that time of year, and Mike made the most of it by offering them a good meal and spooky stories about local ghosts and other things that go bump in the night. In fact, one of my stories involved Mike Purcell. In the early 1980s, he had opened a fish and chips style restaurant on the wharf at Turner Street in Salem, beside the famous House of Seven Gables. When I went there on a hot and humid early afternoon to sample one of his popular lobster rolls, Mike pointed out a two-story building on neighboring Miller's Wharf, where, he said, he hoped to expand his business. *"If you have time, I'll show you around the building. You'll love it,"* he said, *"It's just like an old ship inside. It's a bit small, but it'll make a great eating spot with lots of atmosphere."*

I took Mike up on his offer and allowed him to escort me through the old wooden building at the foot of Miller's Wharf. The first floor seemed somewhat cramped for a restaurant, but by using the second floor as well, Mike thought it could be profitable. The second floor was truly a surprise, for it looked like the inside of an old ship. *"It is an old ship,"* Mike informed me. *"A sea-going barge that was either sunk or abandoned sometime after the turn of the century, and salvaged by old Herbert Miller and brought here to the wharf. He had it hoisted up here to make a second floor to what was once his summer home."*

"This will make a terrific restaurant," I said to Mike, but he hadn't heard me, for someone from the wharf below had called up to him. I walked on to what was once the stern of the old barge and entered the cozy pilot-house. I wasn't in there for a few seconds when a hollow, gruff-sounding voice, seemingly coming from thin air, shouted, *"Get out of here!"* There was no one else in the room, and all windows were closed tight, so it wasn't an echo from the wharf. The voice had that eerie, beyond-the-grave sound to it. I felt anxiety flood my body, but I didn't move. Had I heard the voice? I wondered, or was my mind playing tricks on me in the heat of the day? I could see Mike at the other end of the building, leaning over the banister and speaking with someone on the wharf, well beyond hearing distance, so I knew it wasn't he who demanded that I leave. It was literally a voice from nowhere and, as I stood there, silently sweating from every pore, it came again. A loud and raspy demand, as if from an echo-chamber: *"Get out of here!"*

I immediately left the pilot-house, walked the length of the building, passed Mike on the balcony and went down the stairs to the wharf. Mike, following close on my heels, asked *"What do you think of the place?"* *"I think your place is haunted,"* I replied matter-of-factly.

Mike never did open a restaurant there, and as far as I know, the place has been abandoned ever since.

Ghosts have always fascinated me, but in all my reading on the subject, I had never been aware of ghosts being able to speak. Marley's ghost, however, did talk to Scrooge—but that was fiction. I had no doubt that I had heard the voice at Miller's Wharf speak twice, so I decided to research the old house. Although Herbert Miller was long dead, I tracked his daughter to neighboring Danvers and spoke with her. Her father had told her as a child about salvaging an old barge, but never mentioned the history of the vessel to her, from which I concluded that any information on what the strange voice could be would probably never be uncovered.

Coincidentally, it was while telling ghost stories at Mike Purcell's new restaurant on Washington Street in Salem at Halloween, some ten years later, that more chilling information about the ghostly activity at Miller's Wharf was revealed to me. As usual, some people stay on after my talks to discuss ghostly subjects further, often telling me of encounters with spirits they, or others close to them, have had. One pretty young woman in her mid to late twenties said that *"My husband had an experience much like yours."* Thinking I was going to hear another story about creaky footsteps on the attic stairs, I was amazed when she said that her husband had also heard the ghostly voice at Miller's Wharf, just as I had, but some two years before my experience in the pilot-house. I wanted to hear the story from the source, so I had her lead me to her table in the restaurant where her husband sat eating his dinner. He told me that he was a surveyor who had been hired to measure the property surrounding the wharf.

"There was no one else around," he told me, *"but as my partner and I approached the old house at the foot of the wharf, a raspy, whispery voice growled at us to 'Get out of here!' The voice came from the house, and it had an unearthly tone to it. We looked at each other,"* said the surveyor, *"but since no one came out of the house to confront us, we continued on with our work. A few moments later, the voice repeated, 'Get out of here!' and it seemed louder the second time. So, we picked up our gear and returned to the office. When we got there, my boss was furious that we had left the job. I told him that someone in the house had told us to get out of there; my boss then informed us that nobody lived in the house, nor had anyone lived there for a long time. I was so happy to hear about your encounter in the old house,"* he told me, *"for I really thought I was going batty until I learned about your experience with the talking ghost."*

This revelation by the surveyor convinced me to dig deeper into the mystery. I didn't think returning to the house or attempting to hear the voice again would prove anything, but some hard research at the local library on barges that plied these waters just after the turn of the century, I thought, might provide me with some essential clues on why an old barge might be haunted. What I wasn't prepared for was that there were hundreds of such barges voyaging up and down the North Atlantic, from Pennsylvania to New England, carrying coal during the early 1900s, most being towed three at a time by a tug, and that quite a few had met disaster. The barge that Miller salvaged was in good shape, either left a derelict, or sunk in shallow water for easy salvage. To purchase a seaworthy barge and make it into the second story of a house hardly seemed practical, especially considering that Captain Herbert Miller was reputed to be a frugal old seadog. His daughter, Helen Cooke of Danvers, seemed to remember that Miller had once said the barge was salvaged from Salem or Boston Harbor, possibly a derelict. But anyone could see for themselves, by visiting the house, that the barge was in good shape, with not a sign of rot or repair in it—why then would a perfectly seaworthy barge be abandoned?

During my many years of off and on library research, I discovered that there were three barges heading for Salem and Portsmouth on January 6, 1911, all being towed by the tug LYKENS in heavy seas and strong winds. The three towlines, or hawsers, parted as the tug rounded Cape Cod. All three barges, the CORBIN, TREVORTON, and PINE FOREST, couldn't maneuver on their own, even though each had a captain and crew, and could have easily sailed to safety if the weather had been calmer. All three smashed into the sandy surf off the Cape; the CORBIN and TREVORTON collided with each other and sank side by side with all hands lost. The PINE FOREST touched bottom some 500 yards from shore, and her five-man crew attempted escape in a dory. It capsized and all drowned. In all, 17 barge-men lost their lives. I wondered if possibly it was one of these barges that Miller had salvaged for the second story of his house at the wharf. They had been headed for Salem, and the tragedy of lives lost could possibly account for the outspoken haunting spirit in the pilot-house. The PINE FOREST had remained in one piece during the storm, but there was no mention in the old records as to whether or not she was salvaged. I searched further, mainly into marine magazines, logs, and newspaper records of the time. There were other barges lost in heavy seas, but all, it seemed, had sunk into deep water—and in those days, salvage techniques and cost made it all but impossible to salvage a ship from deep water.

One tragic event, however, concerning a three-masted barge named GLEN-DOWER, soon convinced me that it was probably she that became the second floor dwelling for the ghost at Miller's Wharf. I found no proof of this, but she had been heading for Salem and Newburyport on the fateful evening of June 9, 1911, and had been forced into Boston. There was no furious storm that evening, only a strange situation that forced her in. At about 8:00 p.m., the captain of the tug MONACACY, towing the barges BAST, GLENDOWER and RUTHERFORD, all carrying coal, was notified that not all was well. The crewmen of the GLENDOWER had signaled the tug that their barge captain, Charles Wyman, was dead. Captain Camp of the tug ordered all the barges into Boston, sailing under their own power, and he unhitched the long tow lines to each barge. The tug captain understood from the crew of the GLENDOWER that their skipper had been found dead in his bunk. Captain Camp assumed the 55-year-old Wyman had died in his sleep of natural causes, but when docked at Commercial Wharf, Camp boarded the barge and found Wyman face down in his bunk, covered from head to toe with blood. He immediatly contacted the Boston police and the three crewmen of the GLENDOWER were placed under arrest, each suspected of murder. None of them were Americans; Bill Nilsen was an old deckhand from Norway, Antonio Priskich was an Austrian barge donkeyman, and William De Graff a Dutch cook. The latter was crippled and hunchbacked, and obviously quite disfigured, for a Boston newspaper reporter described him as "a great ugly ape." None of these seemed like murderers to the general public, and there seemed to be no motive for such a horrible crime. The medical examiner reported that Captain Wyman had been viciously hacked to death with an axe; there were over 27 deep wounds to his head and body. There was blood spattered all over his cabin, yet none of the crewmen had blood on his clothes, nor was a bloody axe found aboard the barge. All of them told authorities that they hadn't seen their captain since he went into his cabin after lunch to take a nap. *"When he didn't wake for supper at five, when it was his turn to take the wheel,"* Antonio Priskich testified in broken English, *"I opened his cabin door to find him dead in his bunk, covered with blood. There was blood everywhere. On the walls too. When I screamed, De Graff came and told me not to touch anything, and we closed the door and signaled the tug that we had trouble aboard."* Since none of the crewmen appeared to be murderous men, it was thought that there might have been a stowaway aboard who could have possibly jumped ship or swum ashore once the barge reached Boston. Asa French, the District Attorney of Suffolk County, thought differently. He concluded that De Graff was the murderer. *"He was the only one that could have done it,"* said French. After lunch on the day of the murder, Priskich had relieved Nilsen at the wheel at 2:00 p.m., and both had been on deck most of the afternoon, or so they reported. De Graff, on the other hand, was below all afternoon, his room only some 16 feet from the captain's cabin. Yet De Graff said he heard no sound from the captain's cabin all afternoon. The medical examiner determined that the captain had been killed between 2:00 and 3:00 p.m. Nilsen, at the wheel at that time, testified that he thought he heard a muffled scream of pain from below at about two o'clock, and just prior to that time he thought he heard the captain shout, *"Get out of here!"*

The De Graff murder trial was held in Boston in the midst of a great February blizzard. The noted attorney John Feeney defended the hunchback, and although one barge-man named Axel Hansen testified he once heard De Graff say that *"Captain Wyman is no good,"* this seemed little motive for murder. After long deliberation, the jury verdict was Not Guilty. "The great ugly ape," as the press had dubbed him, disappeared and was never heard from or seen in these parts again.

The barge, because of its horrid history, never went to sea again; as far as anyone knows, she rotted at dockside. I, however, think it was this barge that Herbert Miller purchased for pittance, towed to his wharf in Salem, some 12 miles away, and winched up to make a second story for his summer home. It is, I believe, the spirit of Captain Charles Wyman that haunts Miller's Wharf. His final words, shouted at the hunchback when he entered the captain's cabin with a concealed axe, are forever on his lips. For there is no doubt in my mind that it was "the ugly ape" De Graff who murdered the captain and got away with it—and perhaps, after all, it was deserved justice for both men. Two years after the trial, it was revealed by a Philadelphia seaman named John Breen, under deposition, that *"De Graff had specifically gone to Newburyport from Philadelphia to join the GLENDOWER crew as cook, for the sole purpose of murdering Captain Wyman. His motive stemmed from twenty years before the murder, when Wyman was a deck officer aboard a Maine schooner: Wyman had physically flogged a young seaman out of the ship's rigging in a rage, causing him to fall to the deck, crippling him for life. That seaman was De Graff."* He had waited over twenty years for his revenge. Captain Wyman hadn't recognized De Graff as the seaman whose life he had ruined; and now, it seemed, must spend an eternity in fear of "the great ugly ape," forever challenging all who now approach the haunted GLENDOWER, permanently anchored to the wharf as part of an abandoned house in Salem Harbor.

"The launching of the 680-foot monster GREAT EASTERN in 1857. She was four times bigger than any ship in the world, and she was haunted. Her ghost was uncovered in 1889."

II
THE GREAT EASTERN GHOST

He was known as "the Little Giant," and the ship he built was called "The Monster." Isambard Kingdom Brunel, and Englishman of French origin, had become a noted engineer before he turned thirty years old. He designed and engineered the Great Western Railway, designed and built the famous paddle steamer GREAT WESTERN, as well as the first iron steamship, GREAT BRITAIN. Before he turned fifty, Brunel decided to outdo himself and built the greatest ship afloat: a 680-foot monster that had both screw prop and paddle-wheel propulsion, with three masts to carry sail if necessary. She could accommodate 4,000 passengers; in 1857, she was four times bigger than any other ship in the world.

To say the Brunel's "Monster," GREAT EASTERN, was a jinxed ship right from her day of launching would be an understatement. With thousands watching, she sped down the gangrail with such speed and power that her holding chains and cables parted, sending the windlass spinning out of control in reverse, striking twelve workers. They were hurled above the crowd, as if fired by a rocket. Two of them died and the others were seriously injured. It caused the crowd and many of the workers to panic. Brunel quickly applied the brakes on the launching gear, bringing his ship to a grinding halt well before she hit the water. Then, hard as he tried, Brunel could not get the GREAT EASTERN to budge. More chains and cables parted, hydraulic rams burst, and anything that could go wrong, did. Brunel could only get the great ship to move a few inches each day. It took three months before the ship hit water, the launch costing the Eastern Steam Navigation Company $5,000 per foot. Local contractors were boasting, *"We launched the GREAT EASTERN, and the GREAT EASTERN launched us."* Before she hit the ways, there was another catastrophe: a sightseer's gallery, constructed on a rooftop beside the launching rail, collapsed under the weight of hundreds of onlookers, falling some sixty feet to the ground. There were many broken bones and smashed heads, but no deaths.

"As she slid grandly past," wrote a reporter for the London Times, *"thousands upon thousands crowded to the water's edge with an outburst of enthusiasm and delight...Within ten minutes of being cast off from the tugs, she set at rest forever all doubt as to her being the fastest vessel beyond compare in the world."* The reporter failed to mention that, *"as she passed,"* the GREAT EASTERN also launched many other smaller ships in the vicinity, swamping and sinking most of them, the salvage of which was an added cost to the Eastern Steam Navigation Company. She was the biggest and the fastest, but she was also fast becoming the most expensive ship afloat. During her final inspection before heading to sea, members of her 400-man crew noticed the great change in Brunel as he toured the ship looking for flaws. He was

extremely pale and had lost most of his hair from worry during the long launch. Halfway through the inspection, he collapsed, and had to be carried ashore to the hospital. It was later determined that he had suffered a stroke.

On the day the GREAT EASTERN was to leave the Thames River on a test run, her Captain Harrison was utterly frustrated, for furniture and other bric-a-brac was still coming aboard in dribs and drabs; the bridge telegraph, necessary to announce orders to the aft wheelhouse, had not been installed, and riveters had still not completely sealed the bulkheads. A day later it was reported to the captain by the ship's boatswain that one of the riveters was missing and that some of his fellow workers thought he might have mistakenly sealed himself into the double-bottomed hull. Crewmen reported that they heard faint cries for help from deep within the ship, and a tapping from behind the steel skin of the hull. Harrison conducted a search of every crease in the ship, but the missing riveter was not found. The tapping and moaning from inside the hull, however, continued; or so some crewmen reported.

On the test run, off Hastings, the great ship suddenly shuddered under an enormous explosion that blew out the forward funnel and shattered every floor to ceiling mirror in the plush saloon. Glass flew in every direction, but miraculously, neither crew nor passengers were in the saloon at the time. The only one close by was the captain's little daughter, but she had been playing behind a bulkhead, which protected her from the blast. Steam had built up in the funnel-jacket, causing the explosion, which the London Times called *"the most terrific explosion a vessel has ever survived,"* but there were crewmen who didn't survive it. Fifteen men in the ship's stokehole had been blown up. All were terribly burned and five died. In addition, a fireman in the boiler room jumped overboard to avoid being scalded, but he was caught up in the paddlewheel and crushed to death. Brunel, recuperating at home, suffered yet another stroke when told the news of the explosion and resulting destruction, and dropped dead.

To add to the dilemma of the ship owners, over half the crew mutinied just prior to her maiden voyage to America. The owners brought the strikers to court and won, the ringleader receiving two months in jail and thirty others confined to hard labor for two weeks. The owners then fired most all the crew, and had a difficult time replacing them with experienced men; one inexperienced newly hired engine-fitter had his hand town away in the paddle engine. Soon after the mass firing, a terrible storm, considered one of the most powerful to ever hit England, struck at Holyhead where the GREAT EASTERN was moored. She broke her mooring cables and, as the saloon skylights were blown away in the wind, the monster drifted aimlessly in the pounding surf. Captain Harrison, however, saved the day by getting the engines going and headed the ship into the storm to ride it out without further damage. Close by at Anglesea, the great steamer ROYAL CHARTER, which was arriving from Australia, smashed into the high cliffs with a loss of 446 lives. A few days later, Captain Harrison, the ship's surgeon, the chief purser's nine-year-old son and seven crewmen were coming ashore from the "monster" in the ship's tender, when the boat capsized in a sudden squall. Captain Harrison, the boy, and one crewman drowned.

Eight American and Canadian coastal cities vied for the GREAT EASTERN to dock at their respective ports. Portland, Maine, even built a large pier specifically for the monster ship to dock, but the GREAT EASTERN owners decided on New York as the ship's port-of-call. The Portland city fathers cried foul, and sued the ship company. The New York Herald editor commented: *"What would the GREAT EASTERN do in Portland? Why, in two trips to Europe she would take away the whole population of that enterprising city, leaving its streets as deserted as Pompeii, and in six months she would denude the entire state of Maine of all it's products and manufactures."*

On June 17, 1860, when the great colossus was finally ready to cross the Atlantic, New York Times writer Alexander Hooey wrote: *"The monster struck out for the New World...the final embarkation, the real trip, the first ocean voyage of a ship that has been the parent of more talk, speculation and wonder, and worldwide interest than any craft since Noah's Ark."* Already considered a hard-luck haunted ship in England, there were only 35 paying passengers aboard the monster when she left for America, and the crew numbered 418. Of the thirty-five, fourteen passengers reported to the ship's officer of the day that they had either heard the periodic tap-tap-tapping of a hammer from deep within the bowels of the ship, or a constant ghostly moaning from behind the walls of their cabins, all the way across the Atlantic. Was the sealed-in riveter still trying to find his way out?

Thousands came to watch her maneuver New York Harbor. The New York pilot, Commodore Murphy, commented that *"Every spot where a human being could stand, was covered."*

The GREAT EASTERN had never been berthed before, and when she squeezed into the wooden wharf, it began to crack. The stevedores couldn't handle the mooring lines, so people in the crowd helped out, bringing the great ship to a squeaking halt, but not before her paddlewheel chewed up five feet of the wharf, causing many onlookers to be trampled. When city worker Thomas Learill came to inspect the damage done by the paddlewheel, he fell off the wharf to his death; when a drunken sailor tried to inspect the damage, he too disappeared beneath the wheel, and didn't come up until weeks later, when the paddlewheel scooped him from the muddy bottom as the ship left port.

To recoup all their losses, the ship owners decided to charge admission to tour the ship while she was in port, and the response was encouraging, although the owners charged one dollar per visit, whereas admission to Barnum's Museum down the street was only twenty-five cents. To their dismay, the owners discovered too late that most of the visitors who paid the dollar were taking home souvenirs from the ship of far greater value. Many things that were nailed down, and most things that were not, were absconded. Tourists also let it be known to the press and to the officers and owners of the ship that they found the British crew to be quite surly and nasty. The crew members were also fighting amongst themselves again. A fight erupted in the boiler room one day, in which thirteen crewmen were seriously injured and one was killed. A few days later a fireman named Bill Hicks hit engineman Tom O'Brien with a wrench and killed him. The New York police were called in to remain aboard the ship to maintain order until she left port.

A week before the monster departed, Harper's Weekly summed up her short stay in America: *"She has certainly attracted a great deal of attention, more than any other ship that has ever anchored in the Bay of New York. At the same time it would not be correct to say she has been a success, or that we part with her with very much regret. The managers were grossly inefficient, the ship dirty, the officers and crew discourteous and rude, and Americans who made helpful suggestions were ignored and insulted."*

The GREAT EASTERN departed New York without fanfare and with only 100 passengers. To add insult to injury, the New York Sheriff boarded the ship before she left the harbor with a fistful of warrants—the Brits had not paid all their bills, and were hard pressed to do so—the monster had not yet turned a profit and was sucking in heavy debt at every spin of her paddlewheel. The ship headed for Canada where the owners expected bigger bucks and kinder treatment, but at Halifax, before docking, the ship master was obliged to pay "lighthouse dues" based on tonnage, of $1,750.00 The ship owners thought the Governor of Nova Scotia should pay the fee, but he refused. In a huff, and without the benefit of one new sightseer or passenger, the owners demanded that the ship leave immediately for England. In her haste to make record time across the Atlantic, the engine screw shaft collapsed from overwork, and the monster, for the first time, was forced to sail into port.

With only one round-trip passage under her belt, the GREAT EASTERN had earned the reputation of being a jinxed, hardluck ship, responsible for 22 deaths and many mishaps. Also, accounts of seeing and hearing the ghost of the missing riveter persisted through reports made to the captain and owners by passengers and crewmen alike. This continuing rash of bad luck and strange phenomena manifested itself during the second voyage to New York as well, when halfway across the Atlantic the ship encountered a vicious hurricane. She limped into port after a grueling nine and a half days crossing, but few took notice, and no crowds were there to greet the ship. The Civil War was just a month old, and Americans had other things on their minds—the biggest and fastest ship in the world was a thing of the past. Even at twenty-five cents, few people visited the ship at dockside. She returned to England, where ship owners persuaded officials of the British government to hire the GREAT EASTERN as a troop ship so that they might recoup some of their losses. Under command of a thirty-year-old captain, James Kennedy, the ship sailed for Quebec, Canada, with 2,600 military passengers and 122 horses. Because the ship was lacking some 100 crew members, Kennedy sent out press gangs to local pubs to force British citizens to serve as crew for the crossing to Canada. As the ship was under way, these pressed seamen mutinied. This was the fourth such mutiny aboard the GREAT EASTERN, a record number of crew uprisings, never surpassed by any other ship afloat. Kennedy squelched the mutiny by having his troops fix bayonets and chase the mutineers into the rigging, where he kept them at dagger points all day and all night until they surrendered with cold and fatigue. It was also the first time in history that six stowaways were discovered in the bowels of a ship—all of them female. Aside from the near collision with the Cunard liner ARABIA in the fog off Nova Scotia, *"missed by the length of a bowsprit,"* wrote the <u>London Times</u>, two of the cavalry horses stabled on deck died of the cold, and one sailor, James Pollard, was killed in an accidental fall from the rigging to the deck—otherwise the delivery of troops by the GREAT EASTERN to Canada was uneventful, but the British government never hired the monster again, and her next voyage to North America was one that no one would soon forget, especially the ship owners, for it cost them a fortune.

It was another hurricane that battered the ship as she cruised some 300 miles off the west coast of Ireland. *"Even the oldest sailors could not get their sealegs,"* reported the new Captain Walker, *"as the ship rolled very heavily."* Because the heavy seas were breaking apart the paddlewheel, Captain Walker was obliged to stop the engines at the height of the storm. Without paddle power, the six-ton screw prop could not keep the ship on her heading, and she began to drift sideways into the heavy swells. The captain attempted to raise her sails but the canvas ripped to shreds. Of the 832 aboard, over half were seriously injured, their limbs bruised or broken by rolling chairs, tables, pianos and cargo barrels. Fish oil casks which were part of the cargo broke loose and filled the ship with oily slime and an unbearable smell. Almost every cabin was flooded. *"The scene defies all description,"* wrote one passenger. *"Water has got in to float even the larger articles in the baggage room. The rocking of the ship has set the whole mass in motion. Friction has reduced portmanteaus, hatboxes, dressing cases, and all personal chattels of four hundred passengers into a mass of pulp..."* It was at this point that the crew working the pumps and boilers below went on strike, confiscated all food supplies, and refused to serve the ship or her passengers in any way. The passengers organized a vigilante committee in response. One of its leaders was Hamilton Towle, who convinced the captain that he could jury-rig a hand-made steering contraption to the broken rudder and, with limited prop power, could direct the ship to port in Ireland.

The contraption worked, saving the ship, her passengers, and her rebellious crew. Off Cobh, Ireland, Captain Walker sent off a telegram to the owners in London: *"Having lost both paddles and rudder-head in a terrific gale, I have been compelled to put back under a distress flag into Queenstown."* As they entered Cobh, the GREAT EASTERN smashed into an American bark that was also seeking shelter, causing the quartermaster to strike his head so hard on a beam that he died from the blow. The ship owners rushed to Ireland with cash in their pockets to pay off passenger claims in an effort to avoid more bad publicity and court costs. The paddlewheel was replaced, and by the spring of 1863, the GREAT EASTERN was heading for New York once again. Coincidentally, on the day she arrived, May 17, Hamilton Towle was the toast of the town, receiving a gold medal and the acclaim of thousands for his *"ingenious contrivance of a steering machine, which he fitted to the steamship GREAT EASTERN under circumstances of great peril, and subsequently a complete success in saving numerous passengers and that great ship,"*—so read the plaque he received from the New York Life Saving Benevolent Association. The news coverage brought the monster to the spotlight again, and crowds came to visit her, numbering over 3,000 people each day; when she was ready to return to England, she carried 700 paying passengers. Her near destruction off the coast of Ireland had inadvertently brought financial success, it seemed, but the dark cloud that shadowed her since launching caused an unexpected financial pinch to her owners. Hamilton Towle was suing them $100,000 for salvage rights—after all, he saved the ship, and he deserved a reward. He also reminded the owners that, in their haste to pay off passenger claims in Ireland, they had never thought to take a moment to thank him for saving their ship. It was an oversight that cost the owners a large sum of money in settlement out of court.

Heading into the Atlantic, the GREAT EASTERN met yet another heavy gale, and the new captain, Walter Paton, decided to head back to New York rather than allow the ship to be buffeted by another storm. Instead of entering New York Harbor, he anchored the ship off Montauk Point, then asked for a pilot to lead her into Flushing Bay. In the dead of night the crew and passengers heard and felt the ship hit bottom. Although it was only a slight bump and thud, the great ship was listing to starboard. Peter Falcon, a New York helmet diver, was hired to check the bottom, 26 feet below the waterline; to Captain Paton's dismay, he reported a deep gash in the metal, nine feet wide and eighty-three feet long. Although the bottom was double-hulled, and there was no leakage into the ship's hold, the rip had to be repaired before traveling back out to sea. There wasn't a drydock in America that could handle a ship her size, nor could she be careened anywhere up or down the coast due to her flat bottom. It was finally decided that a cofferdam or iron plates would have to be built all around the ship—a very costly and timely endeavor, but the captain and owners had no other choice.

Once built, riveters would enter the cofferdam each day to repair the hull, and each day diver Falcon would inspect the cofferdam for leaks outside, some 27 feet below the surface. One day while below, he pulled the emergency cord and was quickly brought to the surface. When his tenders removed his helmet, he shouted that he had encountered the ghost of the old riveter. *"He's hammering inside the hull,"* cried the frightened diver. Hearing Falcon, the riveters refused to go below in the chutes to do their work, deciding that the hammering of their long-entombed compatriot was a warning of some future peril. A noted New York spiritualist named Seth Thomas was called in to exorcise the ship and drive off the ghost, but instead, this ghost-buster informed the captain and crew that *"the riveter in body and spirit is inside the ship and will hammer at the hull for eternity."* Captain Paton, angry at the delays and disgusted at the mass hysteria of his workers, called them all *"superstitious fools,"* and jumped into the cofferdam shaft himself to prove to them that there was nothing to fear. He returned to the surface shortly, stating that he too had heard the hammering of what he called *"the spectral basher."* Even the cofferdam designer and builder, Edward Renwich, went below and returned to report that, *"I heard it too, something continuously pounding on the hull from the inside."* The captain had the hull inspected inside and out, but no one could discover where the sounds were coming from, only that it was from somewhere below the waterline. The captain was at a loss for what to do, and so after a week of inactivity he decided to end his ghost problem by telling a lie. He gathered all the workers together and said that he had found *"a swivel hitting the side of the ship just below the waterline, and that is what is making the tapping sound. So, let's stop this foolishness and get back to work."* Some didn't believe him and left the job, and although enough riveters remained to complete the patch, it took until December.

Because of the ghost activity, there was renewed interest in the ship, and when she was ready to sail on New Year's Day, she carried 1,200 passengers. In addition to reviving the ghost of the riveter, and the long delay, the unscheduled stop at Montauk Point, Long Island, had cost the company $350,000, which was Renwick's bill for fixing the leak. On the way back to England there was another death aboard the GREAT EASTERN, and on the same day there was a birth. Captain Paton's wife had a baby boy, and named him James. In later years he was to become Lord Mayor of Southport, England, and was knighted by the Queen.

To save the owners from bankruptcy, the GREAT EASTERN was converted from a passenger ship to a cable laying ship, under the direction of the noted Cyrus Field. He packed 3,000 miles of thick cable aboard her broad deck in

1866, and successfully laid the first underwater Atlantic cable from North America to Europe. The GREAT EASTERN went on to submerge five more transatlantic cables from one continent to another, but because she was too big to enter many harbors and shallow bays, she was up for auction again within a few years. She was purchased by the French government, who tried to transfer her back into a luxury passenger steamer. Famous author Jules Verne was aboard during her first voyage to New York under the French flag. He recorded an accident aboard, much like the one that occurred the day she was launched in England. *"The capstan snapped while dropping an anchor,"* wrote Verne in his journal, *"spinning the capstan, and five men were swept away, struck by the capstan bars, killing four...These unhappy men killed,"* he wrote, *"were only tools, which could be replaced at little expense."* Halfway across the Atlantic, the GREAT EASTERN met a hurricane, which she seemed prone to do on almost all her voyages. Verne wrote about its destruction and the seasick passengers, but what intrigued him most during the storm was a large shipment of dolls that had broken open and spilled. *"New spars covered the sea,"* he wrote, *"and amongst them were thousands of dolls, which my countrymen had thought to acclimatize in America. The little ladies, torn from their cases by the sea, danced on the summits of the waves."* It took thirteen days for the ship to make New York, and Verne witnessed another sailor's death on board, thought to be caused by chronic sea-sickness. Verne attended his shipboard funeral. Battered and wet, Verne watched the North River pilot board the great ship at New York. He carried a black umbrella, which Verne thought strange. He also called the GREAT EASTERN nothing but *"a vast toy."* The pilot's name was Herman Melville, who later wrote the novel Moby Dick, about another monster from the sea. It was the only time these two great writers met, but the meeting meant nothing to either.

Less than 190 passengers could be recruited to take the return voyage to France, even though the Paris Exhibition was in full swing. When she reached port, she went back into receivership. The GREAT EASTERN returned to England and was finally sold for scrap. One would think that this was the last to be heard of this cursed, ill-fated giant of a ship, but it wasn't. She hit the headlines again in May of 1889, when the wreckers who were tearing her apart for scrap mutinied and began fighting amongst themselves over salvage; one wrecker went so far as to split open the skull of another man. Even in her death-knell, the GREAT EASTERN crew were at each others' throats, but more amazing news came soon after, which spread quickly around England and the world, giving everyone a shiver or two. David Duff, a scrap worker aboard the GREAT EASTERN, reported: *"We were breaking in a compartment in the inner shell on the port side, when a shriek went up that stopped all work. We found a skeleton inside the ship's shell. It was the skeleton of the old basher (riveter) who was missing."*

III
THE TERRIBLE TEAZERS

Over the centuries at sea, especially during the days of wooden ships and sails, natural phenomena was often mistaken for the work of the Devil or of angels by superstitious sailors. A good example of this is Saint Elmo's Fire, also called Saint Elmo's Dance, or Corpo Santo, which is nothing more than sparks of electricity in a humid atmosphere being attracted to iron fittings aboard ships; but these dancing flames or sparks were once considered quite evil by sailors of some nations, while others believed them to be the result of angelic visitations. These eerie lights usually appear before storms, dancing about the vessel, and can cause fright to those who have little or no knowledge of what causes them. For hundreds of years, the fishermen of Portugal and Brittany believed that if Saint Elmo's fire alighted on their vessel it meant that they and their ship would survive the upcoming storm.

There is, however, another somewhat similar, but much larger, phenomenon at sea that cannot be as easily explained. Even today, in our supposedly scientifically advanced society, it is considered by most who have seen it to be a haunting specter. Commonly referred to along the New England coast as the "Death Light,", in Nova Scotia it is called the "Teazer Light." It is usually seen a mile or two off shore at or near the time of a full moon, and appears as a large, swiftly moving ball of fire. Some who have come close to it say it has a buzzing sound like a great swarm of bees. Fishermen and seaside dwellers who have seen it more than once say that it is always heading towards shore, and seems to skip across the surface water, disappearing before it touches land. At Pond Cove, Maine, however, where the ball of fire appears at least once a year in midsummer, it has been known to *"twirl about on shore."* Historian Charles Skinner tells us that it always *"rushes in from the sea and buzzes the same seaside house, of a man named Tom Wright, settling on the roof."*

Skinner says that the light first appeared in the early 1800s when a Maine fisherman named Jack Welch disappeared at sea, and that the light reappears each year where Jack was last seen fishing. Only recently, three men fishing in Jack Welch's old spot on a foggy late afternoon, saw *"a ball of light fly directly over us as we fished the channel. It came with a rushing sound and flew inland through the mist. One man, Jennings, fell into the boat trembling."* The ball was described as almost as big as an automobile. That same afternoon, others saw it *"whirling about near shore,"* and then *"hovering over that same old seaside house, once owned by Tom Wright. It seemed to settle on the roof, but disappeared before dark."*

Legend has it that when Tom Wright first saw the light, while he was living there in the 1800s, he ran away, leaving his wife and children, and was never seen in those parts again. Writes Skinner, *"Twenty years later, his widow received a letter signed by Tom from Australia on his deathbed. He confessed to killing Jack Welch, who had been her boyfriend before she married Tom. Wright had crept up on him while he fixed his nets at his mooring, struck him and sailed to sea to dispose of the body with an outgoing tide, then Tom returned to court and marry Welch's girl."* It was what they call *"The Jack Welch Death Light,"* that frightened Tom Wright away, but even after Tom's death, the great ball of flame returns each year to Pond Cove, flies up the channel and buzzes the old house. Is it just some kind of natural phenomenon like Saint Elmo's Fire, nothing more than a ball of electrical sparks?—or is it, as the folks from Maine will tell you, the specter of the murdered fisherman Jack Welch?

Further up the coast, where winters are longer, the tides higher, water colder, and the folks a bit more superstitious, there's hardly a soul north of Liverpool or south of Halifax that hasn't seen the "Teazer Light." It is described as the same in every respect as the "Death Light" of Maine, and began appearing off the Nova Scotian coast at about the same time in the early 1800s.

"It starts as a little ball of light and then quickly grows into a great mass of flames, looking like a ship exploding at sea," says old Joe Clarke of Lunenburg, overlooking Mahone Bay, Nova Scotia. Joe, a skeptic who had been brought up on stories of the *"Teazer Light,"* finally saw the spectacle himself one early evening as he entered his 60th year. *"It looked exactly like a sailing ship all aflame, coming in towards Borgal's Point. I always thought they were old wives' tales, but there she was in all her glory, just before dusk, a great ball of fire just above the surface waters, and it lasted for quite a few minutes, then disappeared. Others with me saw it too."*

Canadian historian Helen Creighton says that the old people living around Mahone Bay don't take lightly the stories of "Teazer Light" sightings. *"They would tell about the apparition sailing to within a couple of yards of boats and filling them with fear because they were sure they would be run down. In one case a fisherman told how she stood directly in his way and he could hear the ropes creak in the blocks. From Boutilier's Point it was reported that the ropes were all on fire. It has been seen coming to East Chester from Quaker Island at two o'clock in the morning. Again some St. Margaret's Bay men were in a boat near Clam Island when they had to get out of the TEAZER's way, and they said they could see crew in the rigging. I have never heard of any calamity following the appearance of the 'Teazer Light', but it often seems to have had a frightening effect."*

Captain Joe Hyson, a nonagenarian sailor of Mahone Bay, said he had seen the Teazer Light *"as often as I have fingers and toes. My mother was a Mader from Mader's Cove and she saw it many different times as well, dating back to the last century. One Christmas Eve we were coming back from Halifax in a southeast wind, with a storm coming up, when I saw a big red light coming at us. I was at the helm and shouted to the skipper, 'What's that?' 'It looks like an explosion ahead,' said the skipper, but it weren't; 'twas the Teazer Light."*

The light is often seen before storms and during a full moon, but most always, no matter what the weather or moon be like, it is seen on the evening of June 26th each and every year. This has been true since the year of 1813. It was at that time, in the midst of a war with America, that the people of Mahone Bay witnessed a terrible tragedy. In fact, it was the second such tragedy within seven months, both involving American privateers named TEAZER.

Even though there were 106 British warships stationed at Halifax, Nova Scotia, bold American privateersmen cruised the Canadian coast, attacking merchant ships, absconding with their cargoes, and dodging the heavily armed warships. One of the most successful privateers was the 88-ton TEAZER out of New York. From July through December, 1812, she captured two full-rigged British ships, six merchant brigs and six Canadian schooners, and she carried only two cannons and fifty men. In late December, however, the British flag-ship SAN DOMINGO cornered her on a raid off Halifax, causing her Captain Wooster to surrender, and captured her entire crew. The British then forced the privateersmen to watch as they set TEAZER ablaze, allowing her to burn to the waterline and sink. Captain Wooster and his men were imprisoned, but within a few months were released in a trade of Canadian and British prisoners, and allowed to go home, but with the stipulation and promise that they would never join another privateering crew to battle the British. Most officers, good on their promise, never went to war again, although some crewmen took the chance and fought the British at sea again, but if recaptured and recognized, they were hanged without trial.

The First Lieutenant aboard the TEAZER was Frederick Johnson, a cocky, hard-nosed Yankee who wasn't about to fulfill his pledge to the British enemy, and when a second new schooner was built by Sam Adams to raid the Nova Scotian coast, Johnson signed aboard, again as second in command, although he told Adams that his desire was to be her commander. Instead, Adams chose William Dobson to command the new craft, which he named YOUNG TEAZ-ER. On May 4th, she headed up the coast from New York to harass shipping off Halifax Harbor. In addition to Johnson, almost the entire crew of the YOUNG TEAZER was made up of the crew of the old TEAZER, and they were out for revenge. This new, faster vessel, with it's alligator figurehead, had five guns and 65 crewmen; she could also be rowed if necessary, with 16 long sweep oars, each manned by two men like galley slaves, in the event she became becalmed, or had to row into the shallows to avoid reefs and rocks.

As bold as brass, the YOUNG TEAZER patrolled Halifax Harbor off Sambro Lighthouse, almost under the guns of the British fort there. She captured two brigs and two schooners off the lighthouse within two weeks, manned them with prize crews and sent them packing, cargoes and all, to New York. The 18-

gun brig SHERBROOKE was sent out of Halifax to destroy the YOUNG TEAZER, but the British were outmaneuvered, and the privateer used a fog-bank to elude the larger, heavier armed ship. The privateer then sailed south to Lunenburg, but there met the large British frigate ORPHEUS. Using her sweeps, YOUNG TEAZER snuck into the shallows of Lunenburg, and then Mahone Bay, using the many small islands there to hide her from the bigger ship. Soon, however, the 74-gun man-of-war LA HOGUE came on the scene, the commander of which hated the little pesky gnat-like privateer. Now, even with her sweeps to bring her into shallow water where the battleships dared not venture, she was trapped in Mahone Bay with no way out without passing either of the great British warships. All three were becalmed and sat silently on still waters like figures on a chessboard.

The commander of the LA HOGUE worked his ship in as close as he could to fire a few shots at the YOUNG TEAZER, but he couldn't get her in close enough to make his fire effective. The ORPHEUS dropped anchor a few miles away, facing the cornered privateer, her commander deciding to play a waiting game. It was nearing 8:00 p.m. and darkness. The LA HOGUE lowered five longboats into the water with armed crews, and each boat had a loaded cannon in the bow. They rowed slowly toward the YOUNG TEAZER. Captain Dobson called all his men on deck to decide what they might do—they had few alternatives. Their backs were to the wall, and the captain suggested surrender, but since most of his crew had signed a pledge when captured some seven months earlier that they wouldn't fight again upon penalty of death, they would surely be hanged. First Lieutenant Johnson said that he had the only answer and, without further word, he took a kerosene lit lamp and thrust it into the ammunition room that housed the black powder and all explosives. Few crewmen had time to jump over the rail when the YOUNG TEAZER blew up with a roar that was heard in Maine, and a flash of flames that shot skyward illuminated Mahone Bay and was seen clearly from Halifax. Windows were broken in houses some ten miles away, so strong was the blast. Only seven badly burned crewmen survived, and they surrendered themselves to the Canadians, were imprisoned, and later returned to New York. Three had been members of the first TEAZER crew as well, but were spared the hangman's noose by British authorities. The YOUNG TEAZER, still afloat but barely, was towed to a nearby island. Although burned black and filled with body fragments, the hull was used to expand Mitchell's Store, and the keel was carved into a cross and remains today at the Anglican Church in Chester. Lieutenant Johnson's desperate action was chastised by all: Canadians, British, and Americans alike, including the few YOUNG TEAZER survivors. And every year on June 26th, the anniversary of the great explosion, the flames are seen again in Mahone Bay—and you'll never convince the folks there that it's any kind of natural phenomenon.

"The training ship ATALAN-TA, vanished with her entire crew of cadets. Only a barrel-stave, washed ashore near the grave of the ATALANTE, provided a clue to her destruction."

"The H.M.S. ATALANTE, wrecked by only the sound of a cannon, and her captain and crew, saved by the ghost of a fisherman."

"Of the 95 women and children aboard the S.S. ATLANTIC, only twelve year-old John Hinley survived."

IV
ATALANTE - ATLANTIC

Only a few weeks less than a year from the day the YOUNG TEAZER blew up in Mahone Bay, Nova Scotia, one of the British ships of the naval task force that helped corner her found herself in deep trouble while plying these same waters. She was the 16-gun H.M.S. ATALANTE, a swift dispatch runner, also utilized to blockade the New England coast. Her crew of 134 officers and men was under the command of Captain Frederick Hickey, an experienced sailor who had commanded the ATALANTE for over six years, sailing out of the home port of Halifax. Now, only a few miles from the home port on the early morning of November 10, 1813, the ship was sailing slowly through heavy swells and a thick, soupy fog—not unusual conditions for Nova Scotia in late autumn. Knowing Halifax harbor like the palm of his hand, Captain Hickey realized he was near Cape Sambro and the Sambro Island Lighthouse, the first to be built in Canada by the British in 1758. (The French of Canada had built a light at Louisbourg in 1731.) In the dense fog, the lookout could not see beyond the bow of the ship, so the Captain fired his fog-signal gun, and await-ed a responding signal of a cannon shot from the lighthouse keeper. The watch officer aboard the ATALANTE testified later that, *"between six and eight a.m., five guns were fired from shipboard, and they were not answered, but at quar-ter to nine, the first gun from shore was heard...The reefs in the topsails were shaken out, the royals were hoisted, and the course was north-northeast, for the harbor mouth."* The problem was, however, that the gun which the watch, Lt. George Chalmer, and others aboard, had heard was not from the Sambro Island Light, but from the ATALANTE's sister ship H.M.S. BARROSSA, also lost in the fog. The mistake was a fatal one. The ATALANTE blindly sailed into crushing breakers at a treacherous reef called, ironically, "Blind Sisters."

The ship sank into the frigid boiling seas within ten minutes. The ATA-LANTE carried three boats and, thanks to the quick thinking and cool com-mand of Captain Hickey, all boats got away—18 men in the ship's gig, 42 in the boat tender, and 74 in the cutter—with gunwales almost awash and threat-ening to founder at any moment, they rowed away into the fog. During all this time, eerie music was playing over the ship, and although everyone heard it, no one paid much attention to where it was coming from. As the boats were leav-ing the sinking ship in great haste, a black man in the rigging waved his fiddle and yelled for them not to forget him. *"Throw away your fiddle and dive in,"* cried the captain, *"We'll save you."* The man contemplated departing with his beloved instrument for a moment, then tossed it aside and dove in to the frigid water to swim to the boats, providing a moment of laughter for the destitute seamen. They were all still in desperate trouble, not knowing which way to row and fearing a wave or swell would swamp them at any moment. With the boats tied off to each other, they headed for what they hoped was Halifax harbor.

Cruising on and on for over three hours and feeling hopelessly lost, a small fishing boat with one man in it suddenly appeared out of the fog, sending up a cheer from the ATALANTE officers and crew. *"Can you get us into shore?"* Captain Hickey asked the fisherman. He only smiled, motioned to the captain to throw him a line, and proceeded to tow them all in, taking long sweeps with his oars with motions that seemed effortless. He brought them into Portuguese Cove at the mouth of Halifax harbor, and by two p.m. that afternoon, they were being treated for exposure and fed by the good people of the Cove. The marvel was that, even though the ship was lost, not a soul was killed or seriously injured. In fact, the captain had them all march two-by-two into Halifax Towne, and a report tells us that *"many were shoeless, but there was not a single straggler."*

Although there was a court-martial by the British Admiralty, *"they could not find any blame concerning any officer or any man of the crew, and Captain Hickey was acquitted from blame."* Strangely, however, no one knew who the fisherman was who saved them from further disaster in the fog and led them into Portuguese Cove. Not even the people of the Cove knew who he was. Captain Hickey reported that he was dressed strangely in tri-con, covered with a scarf, tucked under his chin, and a heavy grey great-coat, *"the likes of which most had not seen in these parts for over a century."* ATALANTE crew members commented that although his face seemed *"gruff and swollen,"* yet very pale, *"he wore a perpetual smile"* as he rowed them all ashore with what seemed like supernatural strength. The Cove people concluded that it was Manual Silva, an old Portuguese fisherman who had drowned while out fishing off Sambro Light in November 1763, exactly 50 years earlier.

It was sixty-six years later that another great British ship of a similar name was swallowed up by the sea, but her crew was not as fortunate as that of the ATALANTE. On November 7, 1879, the H.M.S. ATALANTA sailed from Portsmouth, England, heading into the Atlantic. Her commander was Captain Francis Stirling, and her crew was of 300 boys being trained to be sailors. After a stop at Bermuda in January to bring two boys sick with jaundice to the hospital, the ship was to sail back to England and arrive on April 4th. When the ATALANTA didn't show up that day, the entire country began to worry. A fleet of naval ships under Admiral Hood was sent out from England to search the high seas for the missing training ship. They cruised in line for hundreds of miles—never had there been such an all-out search, but no sign of the ATALANTA was found. Strangely, the first possible clue from the overdue ship came from a note in a bottle, picked up by fisherman Ed Millet off Rockport, Massachusetts on June 14, 1880. It read: *"April 17, 1880, training ship ATALANTA. We are sinking in L. 270°, Lat. 32°. Any person finding this note will please advertise in the daily papers. John L. Hutchins. Distress."* Hutchins was one of the young cadets aboard, but the position of the ship he gives in the note would mean that the ATALANTA drifted, or was forced, far off course, possibly in a storm, bringing her south of the Azores. The British gunboat AVON discovered a mass of wreckage while cruising off the Azores at that time, but nothing bore the name of the ATALANTA, and the wreckage was so far from her scheduled route that it was discounted as coming from her. Two days after the note in the bottle was found at Rockport, children playing at Cow Bay, Halifax, Nova Scotia, just eight miles from where the ATALANTE met her end in 1813, found a barrel-stave in the sand with writing on it. The note, written in pencil, read *"ATALANTA going down. April 15, 1880. No hope. Send this to Mrs. Mary White, Sussex—James White."* White was also one of the 300 training seamen. These were the only clues to the possible whereabouts of the 131–foot ATALANTA. The reason for her sinking and why no bodies nor items from the ship have ever been found remains a mystery.

It was April Fools Day, seven years before the ATALANTA disappearance, at that notorious entrance to Halifax harbor, that the worst 19th–century disaster of the North Atlantic coast occurred. It was just another one of those navigational errors—a simple mistake—but it destroyed the great liner ATLANTIC and killed hundreds of people. She was the finest luxury steamer of her day, the pride of the Brits, 435 feet long, and the fastest thing afloat. With four engines and four ship-rigged masts, she could steam or sail across the Atlantic, and she had seven water-tight compartments, making her virtually unsinkable. She sailed from Liverpool with 931 people aboard on March 20, 1873. After a brief stop in Ireland to take on steerage passengers, she sped off to New York. A mid-ocean storm slowed her down, and she began eating up her storage of coal at an alarming rate. Captain John Williams decided that he would have to pull into Halifax for more coal and provisions before heading to New York. He concluded that it would be better to delay passage a day or two than run out of fuel and be forced to sail into New York Harbor.

When Captain Williams caught sight of what he thought was Sambro Island Light, he set a course for some nine miles east of the lighthouse, which would bring the ship into Halifax harbor; but, being unfamiliar with the area, the captain based his sightings on Peggy's Point Lighthouse, which was some 18 miles southeast of Sambro Light. Believing he was in deep water, at 2:30 a.m. Captain Williams went to his cabin to sleep, turning the watch over to his Third Mate, Matt Brady. A half hour later, Brady twisted the wheel hard to port, shouting, *"Breakers! Breakers ahead!"* He was too late to miss the hard jagged peaks jutting from the sea. The great liner shrieked and shivered, then crunched over the reef. With mighty waves breaking over her decks, she shuddered to a halt and began leaning to port. The cold sea filled the water-tight compartments and steerage cabins, killing many of the second and third class passengers.

There was fear, panic, and pandemonium as passengers were rudely shaken from their sleep. Some rushed out on deck in their nightclothes, and were immediately swept overboard by giant breakers. They were in the foaming sea and being hurled against the rocks before they knew what had hit them. As the ship rolled to and fro, listing to a fifty degree angle, all the ship's boats were splintered to matchwood in their davits, or else were swamped, leaving the surviving crew and passengers no means of escape. Captain Williams, now on deck trying to instill some semblance of order, had his officers force many passengers into the rigging to save them from drowning. The ship's great boom broke loose and swung in low, knocking people from the deck and rigging like a massive bowling ball. Within minutes, half the passengers were dead, victims of the raging surf that battered Mars Head, Mosher Island, Nova Scotia, only a few miles from where the ATALANTE was swallowed in the surf in 1813, and near the place where the barrelstave message from the ATALANTA would be found on the beach seven years hence. To those who were still alive, cold and wet, strapped to the rigging or straddling the pitching deck, there seemed no escape.

Third Mate Matt Brady, who had been at the wheel when the ATLANTIC struck, volunteered to sacrifice himself by having a rope tied around his waist and attempting to swim to a large outcropping of rock some 100 yards from the sinking ship, the top of which was high and dry above the breakers. Both Brady and a sailor named Owens tried to make the rock island so that they might tie a line to it, but both failed; although Owens did reach the rock, the waves battered him so violently that he was pulled back to the ship, bloody and nearly unconscious. When Brady admitted that he felt all was lost, another ATLANTIC sailor pointed out that someone apparently had made it to the elevated island rock, for at the top of it, standing and waving, they could see a young lad with long blonde hair flowing over his shoulders. He was naked to the waist, wearing only a tattered pair of pants. Brady couldn't believe his eyes. It wasn't a crewman, for Brady would have recognized him. Was he a passenger, he wondered? But what matter—Brady and the others were elated that the young man's line was made fast to the ship's bow cleat, and the boy on the rock pulled it tight. Then other lines were pulled across to him and tied off to the rock until there were five lifelines that passengers and crew could use to pull themselves across to the safety of the rock. It soon became a human bridge of desperate people, and of the 250 or so that attempted the crossing, only 50 made it to the summit of the rock and dry land. At dawn, the few fishermen living on Meager's Island spotted the survivors and the remains of the ATLANTIC. They came out in boats to attempt a rescue. Some of these heroic fishermen capsized in their boats trying to save passengers. Captain Williams tried to direct the rescuers from the ATLANTIC deck to those who had been hanging most of the night in the rigging, wanting them to be rescued first. Many, unfortunately, had already frozen to death. When the survivors were safely warmed and fed in humble fishermen shacks on the island, the dead were collected for proper burial. There were 546 of them, and when all were accounted for, it was discovered that of the 95 women and children aboard, only a twelve-year-old boy named John Hinley survived.

"I was too confident," said Captain Williams at the court hearing in Halifax. *"I thought I knew where the vessel was. I thought I was a long way eastward of Sambro Light. To think that while hundreds of men were saved, every woman should have perished. It's horrible. If I'd been able to save just one I could bear the disaster, but to lose every woman on board, it's too terrible."* Williams had his captain's certificate suspended for only two years—too lenient a penalty, many surmised, for a man thought to have committed the *"crime of the century."*

Even though he was at the wheel when the ship went down, Third Mate Matt Brady was considered the hero of the day. His rope bridge from ship to rock island showed great ingenuity, gallantry, and almost super-human endurance. Yet Brady insisted that it was not he, but the boy with the long blonde hair, who was the real hero of the day—but it was later determined that there was no such passenger aboard, nor was he an ATLANTIC crewman. No one had seen him swim to the rock or fight his way through the battering surf to the rock summit, and after he had secured the all-important lifeline, no one saw him again. Brady conducted an extensive search to find the young man, but was unsuccessful. It was two months after the great disaster that he received a letter from a widow who lived on Meager Island near the wreck site: *"I have heard that you are looking for the young man who mysteriously appeared out of nowhere on the morning of the wreck, and how he bravely helped the first passengers ashore, and how he disappeared as mysteriously as he appeared. The description of this young brave lad, as described by you and other survivors, fits the like of my own son exactly, even to the long wild yellow hair. Like his Dad, my wonderful young son drowned while out fishing, and was found wedged in the very rocks where the steamer ATLANTIC was grounded and torn to pieces, only a year before. Do you think it could have been the spirit of my son who came to the aid of yourself and the others in your distress?"*

It is not known whether Brady replied to the distressed mother and widow, for her letter was found in his diary many years after he had passed away. Neither is it known if Brady thought the heroic boy was a ghost. After all, as a highly capable naval officer, admitting such supernatural activity was hardly proper in 19th–century society. The tragedy at Mars Head in 1873, however, and the encounter in the fog only six miles away in 1813, might make one consider the possibility of benevolent spirits of fishermen haunting the terrible reefs off Sambro Island Light at the mouth of Halifax Harbor. If not the ghosts of fishermen long gone, then who were these saviors of so many lives aboard ships of similar names?

V
VESSELS THAT VANISHED

A year doesn't go by that we don't read in the newspapers of some ship being lost at sea. Usually she is the victim of a storm or collision, and sometimes there is death involved. Rarely, however, do we read of vessels that vanish, never to be seen or heard from again, with not one of her occupants ever being found and no remnant of her hull or contents left floating on the surface. Some of these vanishing vessels are sailboats or fishing boats, carrying only a few occupants, but on occasion they are great yachts or luxury liners carrying hundreds of people. The causes of these disappearances, of course, remain a mystery, but theorists usually come to one of the following conclusions: the ship was destroyed by a storm, her crew and cargo scattered by currents to the four winds; she collided with a derelict ship or an iceberg, and sank under the waves; or she was top-heavy, struck by a giant wave, turned turtle and sank. Unless one ventures into the paranormal, there seems to be no other explanation for the complete disappearance of a ship and all aboard her. To add to the mystery, certain areas of the ocean seem to be prone to these rare accidents of absolute destruction. The Bermuda Triangle is notorious for a variety of nautical nightmares, including vanishing vessels, but in the North Atlantic, especially off Boston and Halifax, more vessels have disappeared or have been completely destroyed under mysterious circumstances. The Atlantic Ocean off North America is extremely dangerous during the winter months, and most disappearances do occur at that time; still, this doesn't explain why no S.O.S. or distress signals were sent out, nor why not even one life vest is found floating on the surface when a ship disappears. Usually, the surface of the sea is strewn with debris when a ship wrecks, but with these vanishing ships, not even a splinter of wood is found.

Probably the most devastated of America's vanishing fleet are New England fishing boats out of Gloucester and New Bedford, Massachusetts. Every other year, on average, one disappears with all hands lost, usually with not a clue as to what happened to her. The 86–foot trawler CAPTAIN COSMO out of Gloucester is a good example. She left port on September 2, 1978, carrying a crew of six men to trawl the productive fishing grounds some 200 miles east of Cape Cod. During the next few days she was in radio contact with three other fishing vessels, and all seemed well. Captain Cosmo Marcantonio told the captain of the SAINT NICHOLAS that he was going to stay in that area to fish a couple of more days, through September 11th, and that he would then head home; but the CAPTAIN COSMO never returned to Gloucester, and nothing was ever heard of the ship or crew again. There was an eight day search by the Coast Guard and other fishing vessels, plus an air search, including a U-2 spy plane that flew to the East Coast from California. Over 120,000 miles were diligently searched, but not a speck of evidence regarding her whereabouts was ever found. As rare as these complete disappearances might be, less than a year earlier the trawler NAVIGATOR out of New Bedford, with 13 fishermen aboard, also disappeared without a trace, some sixty miles off Nantucket Island. The situation was almost the same as that of the CAPTAIN COSMO. Three other trawlers were fishing nearby, and all were in radio communication, the weather was fine with a choppy sea—and then the NAVIGATOR was gone; no distress signal and without a trace of the ship or her crew. Again, there was an all-out search without any positive results. The secretive sea did, however, provide one clue exactly a month later, on January 8th, 1978, which only added to the mystery. The trawler SECUNDO, 100 miles south of Cape Cod, netted the body of a fisherman in her trawl. It was NAVIGATOR crewman Richard Neild, still dressed in his oilskins. Back in New Bedford, when the coroner undressed the corpse, he found Neild dressed in a suit and tie, hardly the clothes of a fisherman. To this day, no one knows why he was dressed up as if to go to a dance, or a wedding, or a funeral. This was all that the sea ever revealed of the NAVIGATOR. Her loss was the worst tragedy to the fishing community of New Bedford since whaling days.

There was a New Year's Day surprise, similar to that experienced by the crew of the SECUNDO, for Captain Myhre and his men aboard the trawler VEN-TOSA on the first day of 1928. The Gloucester schooner COLUMBIA had been missing for five months. She and her crew of twenty had disappeared in an August storm, leaving not a bit of flotsam behind. Dragging some fifty miles off the coast, Captain Myhre hauled up something very heavy in his trawl from a ninety–foot depth. There, caught up in the three–inch steel cables, was the COLUMBIA, masts erect, mud caking her deck, and what looked like a corpse shackled to the helm. She swayed to and fro, suspended in mid-air at the stern of the VENTOSA. Her captain and crew stared at her wide-eyed until the cables snapped under the strain, and the COLUMBIA sank back into the sea. *"It was as if her captain and crew wanted us to know what had happened to her,"* Captain Myhre said, *"so that we could return to Gloucester to tell their friends and family."*

There was but one female passenger aboard the brig AMARANTH when she sailed from Shelbourne, Nova Scotia to New York on December 18th, 1837. Her name was Margaret Flynn. She, the brig, her captain George Card, and a four-man crew, plus six male passengers, all disappeared without a trace. Thirty years later, Margaret Flynn showed up again, looking as pretty as she did when she stepped aboard the AMARANTH. She was dug up from Mud Island, off the southern tip of Nova Scotia, by curious explorers who found six graves on the desolate island, one of them containing Margaret. She had been placed in a wooden box, so it is obvious that some good Samaritan found her and some of the others washed ashore from the AMARANTH wreck and buried them. Strangely, however, Margaret Flynn's body was perfectly preserved—so well that she could easily be identified by friends and relatives. Mud Island immediately became a tourist site where hundreds came to gawk at Margaret's petrified body. Local resident George Kinney considered it bad taste to display Margaret as a curio; so, out of courtesy, he reburied her in an unmarked grave near his own home. Thus, the spectators soon stopped coming. There never were any answers as to why the AMARANTH sank, nor why Margaret Flynn's body had been so well preserved over the years.

Three years and three months after the AMARANTH disappeared, the greatest sea tragedy of the nineteenth century occurred—the complete disappearance of the luxury steamship PRESIDENT, with 121 people aboard, including famous British actor Tyrone Power. She had left New York for Liverpool on March 11, 1841, and except for a brief gale off New England as she was passing through, there were no major storms reported in the Atlantic. An announcement appeared in the London Times on March 31, stating that the steamship PRESIDENT was overdue. Some people were worried, but most believed that she was just delayed for one reason or another. Seven days later another newspaper report read:

"Nothing whatever has been heard of the PRESIDENT steamer. If she has run to southward, and made for the Western Isles for the purpose of replenishing her coal, she is not yet due. The Liverpool Steamship when, in the winter of 1839 she was compelled to run to the same islands to replenish her coal, took 27 days on the passage from New York to Liverpool. Prevalent opinion is that she must have run to the Western Isles and that she may be expected to arrive in a few days. Indeed, there was yesterday a rumor afloat that the LYNX had seen a steamer making for Fayal..."

There were many rumors running rampant, especially in England. On the morning of April 13th, there was a report out of Birmingham, England, that there was a special train just in from Liverpool with PRESIDENT passengers, and that the steamer had arrived in port. This excited relatives and friends of passengers, but soon proved to be a hoax. A Cork, Ireland newspaper headlined that a note in a bottle had been found on the beach there, which read: *"The PRESIDENT is sinking, God help us all. Tyrone Power."* This, too, was considered by the steamship company to be a hoax. Queen Victoria and Prince Albert, upon leaving Buckingham Palace for Windsor Castle, gave strict orders to dispatch immediate news to them on any information concerning the PRESIDENT. No news was ever dispatched, for there was never any information forthcoming. There have been many theories over the years as to what may have happened, most involving icebergs and derelict encounters, or freak waves that demolished the ship. There has only been one possible clue to her whereabouts, which came almost 100 years later. A beachcomber named John Blake, hiking the cliffs of Hull overlooking Boston Bay, noticed a large plank bobbing off the coast in heavy seas. When a wave washed it in, Blake retrieved it. It was seven feet long and over a foot high. When he turned it over, there were the fading letters PRESIDEN—the "T" was missing. The screws used to fasten the board were corroded, and experts dated them to the mid–1800s. It was concluded that the board was once attached to a wheelhouse that had been underwater for many years. But was it from the long-lost steamer PRESI-DENT, or from another ship of the same name? We'll probably never know for sure; but if so, then the steamer lies on the ocean floor somewhere off the Massachusetts coast, indicating that she probably sank only one day out of New York. But why did not a single piece of her wreckage, or one victim, float to the surface waters or come ashore?

Thirteen years later, almost to the day of the PRESIDENT's demise, another great steamer, the CITY OF GLASGOW, left Liverpool, bound for America with 480 people aboard, 76 of them members of her crew. She was screw-propelled with two 350 horsepower engines. Known for her speed and power, as well as her ability to weather fierce storms, she was considered a safe ship. The weather was perfect, not a stormcloud in the sky. Yet, from the day she left port, March 1, 1854, not a soul saw either her or her occupants again. Other steamers, such as the WESTMORELAND, which left Liverpool at about the same time, encountered no bad weather and arrived at Philadelphia only slightly behind schedule, without ever spotting the CITY OF GLASGOW. Her sister ship, CITY OF MANCHESTER, had left America the same day the GLAS-GOW left England, but they never crossed en route, which alerted the owners that GLASGOW had possibly experienced some accident or mishap forcing her off her normal course. The MANCHESTER captain reported to the steamship owners that she had encountered *"enormous masses of ice along the route,"*; the WESTMORELAND commander announced that his ship had actually been caught in the ice flow, and that he had seen bergs over two hundred feet high off Newfoundland. One ice mass, floating south, he calculated to be 347 miles long. With this information, the only conclusion anyone could come to was that the CITY OF GLASGOW had plowed into one of the giant bergs and sank. However, it seems as impossible then as it does now, that such an enormous ship with 480 people aboard could evaporate into a sheet of ice without leaving some piece of evidence behind, but nothing was ever found from the CITY OF GLASGOW.

Two years later, it happened again: the mail-steamer PACIFIC, steaming between Liverpool and New York, vanished with 188 people aboard. When no word of her was forthcoming and no remnant of wreckage was found, it was concluded that she, too, had met up with an iceberg. But why no evidence, one wonders, even if she did collide? Other ships used this route to America, from Newfoundland to Nova Scotia to New England and New York—why wouldn't they encounter wreckage or bodies, lifeboats or lifebelts, or any other flotsam from these vanished ships?

Eight years to the day of the PACIFIC leaving Liverpool for New York, the 322–foot luxury liner CITY OF BOSTON left the port of Halifax, Nova Scotia, for Liverpool, under the command of Captain J. Halcrow. He was an experienced skipper who had crossed the North Atlantic many times. The CITY OF BOSTON was a mail-passenger steamer, and one of the first of all-iron construction. She was speedy and safe, with two 300–horsepower engines; in the unlikely event that her mighty engines failed, she was also rigged as a sailing ship. Her eight compartments and seven bulkheads were watertight, and her cabins were luxurious, attracting many wealthy voyagers. She had already steamed from ports in England to Boston or Halifax for six years without a mishap. When she departed on January 28, 1870, she carried mail and food-stuffs as cargo, plus 91 crew members and 107 passengers. There were no storms brewing in the Atlantic, and little ice and no fog in the shipping lanes; yet she cruised into oblivion, never to be seen again. No other ships plying the Atlantic saw her afloat, nor came across wreckage or bodies, and nothing drifted ashore along the route. There was but one erroneous report that she was seen sailing into a West Indian island, because her props had failed. This only gave friends a relatives a fleeting glimmer of hope.

Among the missing passengers was a twelve-year-old boy named William Smith, from Detroit, Michigan. His mother refused to believe that her "Young Willie" was dead. She moved to Boston to await her son's return. Every day at meal times, she would set a place at the table for Willie, and she did this until the day she died some thirty years later. As the years went by, friends and relatives had suggested to Mrs. Smith to give up the ritual, but her reply was always the same: *"Willie has not arrived yet, but he is sure to turn up one day this week,"*

The great one-eyed CYCLOPS—the large, cumbersome American Navy coal-collier—couldn't have had a more appropriate name. She was 542 feet long, with a 65–foot beam, and registered at 14,500 tons, but she could travel the high seas at 14 knots, which wasn't too bad for such a massive vessel. As World War I progressed slowly to the Allies' favor, the CYCLOPS was detached from the American Fleet stationed at Hampton Roads, Virginia, and reassigned to Overseas Transportation. On January 8, 1918, she brought a load of coal to Brazil, and on January 28, with a cargo of manganese ore, she sailed for Barbados. On March 4th, she sailed again out into the Atlantic, and hasn't been heard from since. Gone with her was Captain W. Worley and 308 others; 237 crew members and 71 naval passengers. To have such a giant of a ship, with so many naval personnel aboard, simply disappear without a trace provoked an intense military investigation. One of the ship's two engines was having trouble when she anchored off Barbados, and although the engine was repaired, she left the island cruising at reduced speed, and planned to stay fairly close to shore, heading for Virginia before going overseas. It was discovered during the investigation that Captain Worley had changed his name earlier in life, and was once known as George Frederick Wichman, born in Berlin, Germany. Could he have been a German spy and turned the CYCLOPS over to the enemy? Most thought Worley not only a competent commander, but a good American citizen as well, and not one to give up the ship. It was also thought that a German submarine might have torpedoed or captured the CYCLOPS; but after the war, German records showed no U-boats in these waters at that time, and no record of capture or destruction of the great CYCLOPS. Another theory was that the manganese ore she carried as cargo was splashed by saltwater, causing a deadly gas that killed all aboard; but if this were true, why wasn't the ship ever found, or at least some remnant of it? The missing giant CYCLOPS is as much a mystery today as it was then, and although many ships and men were lost at sea during both world wars, none disappeared as completely and mysteriously as the CYCLOPS.

Of all great warships throughout British and American history, none were as gallant or as mysterious as those given the name WASP. In all, there were ten of them, including one which remains afloat, the U.S.S. WASP, aircraft carrier, offshoot to the carrier of the same name which was all but destroyed by a Japanese submarine during World War II, and ultimately destroyed in the autumn of 1942 by an American destroyer to avoid capture by the Japanese. Two other WASPs were gunboats in the Spanish-American War and the Civil War. The first was a 630–ton converted yacht, and the other a steel-hulled steamer, captured from the Rebels off South Carolina in 1863 and used as a special-service dispatch vessel until 1876. Eight years later, the H.M.S. WASP, cruising the West Coast of Ireland, encountered a squall and wrecked on Tory Island. Of the 58 British sailors aboard, only eight survived, the ship being a total loss. On September 9, 1887, another British gunboat WASP, with some sixty men aboard, disappeared at sea for no known reason, with never a clue as to why she vanished, three years to the day the first gunboat WASP sank off Ireland.

The first American WASP was a Revolutionary War privateer, commissioned by George Washington. She was manned by nine sailors from Marblehead, Massachusetts, and often wasn't armed with more than a musket or two. Her one claim to fame is that she was the smallest vessel ever to sail as a warship in the American Navy. She too disappeared with all hands, while out fishing in a September storm. The second American warship WASP was one of the original and official naval vessels commissioned by Congress in 1775. She was an eight-gun schooner, whose first mission was to sail from Chesapeake Bay to the Bahamas, with the PROVIDENCE to assist the first-ever landing of American Marines. Two years later, she was caught up in a storm off Delaware and forced ashore. In order to avoid her capture by the British, she was purposely set afire and burned to the waterline. The next American warship named

WASP was an 18–ton sloop, launched April 21, 1806. She carried 138 men, and constantly patrolled the East Coast of America, looking for smugglers and, during the War of 1812, baiting British warships. Although involved in many battles, the one she is most noted for was her engagement with the British brig FROLIC, which the Americans won during a raging storm by jamming the two ships together and boarding FROLIC in hand-to-hand combat. Over 30 FROL-IC sailors, including her captain, died in the battle, and 50 British tars were badly wounded, with only five WASP sailors killed and five wounded. As the WASP's commander, Jacob Jones attempted to escort the FROLIC into a New England port, the British man-of-war POITIERS intercepted them. She carried 70 guns, and the WASP was no match for her. Jones was obliged to surrender his ship. They all sailed for Bermuda, and the Americans were placed in jail. The WASP, now fighting for the British, was re-named, re-manned, and put back out to sea. Heading for Virginia to do battle, she encountered a storm and sank without a trace, with all hands lost.

The American Navy had a new WASP built and down the ways at Portsmouth, New Hampshire, on May 1st, 1814. Ironically, her sister ship was another sloop-of-war named FROLIC. The WASP, under command of Johnston Blakely and 173 crewmen, was 117 feet long and carried 18 guns. She headed straight for the English Channel and action. Her first battle with the British sloop REINDEER was hot and bloody, with cannons being fired at distances of fifty feet. The contestants were evenly matched, but fire from the WASP devastated the REINDEER, killing her commander and forcing the captain's clerk to give up the ship. The WASP then took on the British brig AVON, which was guarding ten merchant cargo ships, and the Americans were victorious in capturing four of the merchantmen and sinking the AVON, rescuing the British crew before the AVON went down. WASP then captured the British privateer ATALANTA and sent her to Savannah, Georgia, as a prize of war. She arrived in port on November 4, 1814, carrying letters from members of the WASP crew for their families and friends, to be delivered later by mail packet from Georgia to Boston and Portsmouth—these were the last words ever heard from sailors of the WASP.

The great fighting ship WASP disappeared, last seen on October 9th by captain and crew of the Swedish bark ADONIS, somewhere in the mid-Atlantic. There were no storms in the vicinity at that time, the Swedish commander reported, and unless the WASP met up with a heavily armed British man-of-war that sank her without reporting it, there seems to be no reason in the world why she should vanish without a trace. She was a great loss to the American Navy and to the nation. Yet, with two feisty war-sloops of the same name disappearing without a trace less than two years from each other, it's a wonder the American Navy ever named another vessel WASP, but they did just that, and there were four more which all proved to be great sea warriors.

Does the spirit of all these great vanished ships live on, one wonders, destined to ride the waves forever, appearing periodically from behind an iceberg, or through a thick fog, occasionally seen by those in passing ships who wonder if, indeed, they have seen a phantom ship?

The mail-passenger steamer CITY OF BOSTON, with 198 people aboard, disappeared after leaving Halifax, January 28, 1870.

The American frigate WASP battles the British frigate FROLIC off New England during the War of 1812. WASP won the sea battle, but was soon captured by a British man-of-war, and like many of her name, disappeared without a trace.
Watercolor by George Wales, courtesy of the Peabody-Essex Museum.

Caroline Mitchell knew something terrible would happen to the 284-foot luxury liner ARCTIC, and refused to sail on her; her brother did. The ARCTIC collided with the VESTA off Newfoundland and sank on September 27, 1854, with 322 of the 390 aboard her drowning or dying of exposure.

The notorious MARY CELESTE, found abandoned with her cargo intact off the Azores, and her Captain Benjamin Briggs. He disappeared with nine others in November of 1872.
Ship by Rudolph Ruzicka.

VI
PREMONITIONS OF DISASTER

I have had premonitions of incidents which later in life became realities; possibly you or friends of yours have too. They don't happen often, but when they do, they come in a flash and then seem to fade from consciousness. At the time, they seem to have no meaning or sense at all; but hours, days, or even years later, the premonition becomes real. Even then, the reason for this brief glimpse into the future doesn't always seem to make sense. Sometimes these peeks into the future are forewarnings of tragedy and disaster, but often they are of wondrous events. My most vivid premonition came when I was seventeen years old, working for Victor Thomas, a happy-go-lucky oil burner repair man of Salem, Massachusetts. At that time, I was living with my parents in the neighboring town of Marblehead. One day, Victor and I were driving in his work truck down a back road in North Salem. As we passed an old, antique-looking house, I spontaneously said to Vic, *"I'm going to live there some day."*

"Why do you say that?" asked Vic.

"I don't know," I replied, *"but I just know I will live in that house."* The words were out of my mouth without thinking. I had no idea why I said them, but for some unknown reason, I knew that I would someday make that old house my home. Some fifteen years later, married, with a child, and living in Boston, we visited Salem one New Year's Eve and spent the night in South Salem with John Mansfield and his family. The next day was extremely warm for January in New England, and I decided on visiting some of my old haunts where I played as a boy, but my wife was determined to go house hunting, for she was sick of apartment living in Boston. Someone at the party the night before had told her of an old house for sale in North Salem. Sandy was a New Hampshire girl, and didn't know the city, but she managed to find the house and immediately fell in love with it. Before we left Salem for Boston, she begged me to see it, and I complied. We approached the house from the rear, toured the inside with the owner, John Hooper, and then went out in the street to get a good look at the front of the house. Yes, you've guessed it: it was the old antique place that I had told Vic Thomas I'd live in some day, and is where I now sit at the typewriter. I've lived here for over thirty years now. Why I was provided this revelation into my future I do not know; but I consider it a wondrous event, and my wife and I still love the old house, built in 1807, as do our four children who were raised here. It seems that most premonitions, however, come as warnings or predictions of tragedy to be experienced by a loved one, or by the one who is possessed by this momentary, strange sensation. In previous generations, old Yankees called such forewarnings "second sight," or "forerunners of disaster." One of the earliest recorded came to Jeffrey Richardson of Marshfield, Massachusetts, on the evening of March 4, 1787.

Jeffrey was wakened in the middle of the night by the distinct voice of his brother-in-law, Captain Jim Scott, calling to him. Scott, married to Jeffrey's sister Mary, was commander of the brig MINERVA of Cape Cod, due in port from a two-week fishing voyage to George's Bank. Jeffrey considered the anguished cry nothing more than a bad dream, and went back to sleep, to be jolted from his dreams once again only a few moments later by a similar cry of his name, again by a voice he recognized as Jim Scott's. Jeffrey woke his wife to tell her what he heard, and although she didn't think it was anything to worry about, he couldn't get back to sleep. Outside his seaside home, a blizzard was raging. He dressed in his warmest clothes and woke his wife again and told her he was going to the beach. *"There's a noreaster blowing,"* he said, *"and I fear Jim Scott is in terrible trouble."* His wife made him wait until the light of dawn to leave the house, telling him that she thought he was worrying over nothing— *"Jim and the MINERVA have weathered much worse than what is blowing outside."* Struggling through the snowdrifts, Jeffrey reached the beach at about 6:00 a.m., and was greeted by a scene of horror. Bodies and wreckage were strewn on the shore as far as the eye could see. Other locals were now arriving as well, sorting through the wreckage. Parts of a quarterboard were found and pieced together to form the name "MINERVA." Among the dead bodies washed ashore was Jim Scott, his face barely recognizable due to the battering surf. Jeffrey Richardson, questioned many times over the years about the voice he heard the night of the wreck, was always adamant that it had been a "forerunner"—the dying screams of Jim Scott aboard his sinking ship.

Historian Samuel Adams Drake tells the story of elderly grandparents living north of Portland, Maine, in 1817, who *"had a son Tom, crewman aboard the ARGONAUT,"* who, by all accounts, was *"a likable young fellow."* He had recently departed on his tenth voyage, and had left home in a joyous mood, for he had just been promoted to first mate. *"The very day after the ARGONAUT went to sea,"* writes Drake, *"a tremendous gale set in from the eastward. It blew great guns. It seemed as if the gale would never stop blowing. As day after day went by, the storm raged on without intermission...It was on the fourth night of the gale that grandmother and grandfather were sitting together, as usual, in the old family sitting-room, when some great gust came roaring down the chimney to fan the embers into a fierce flame. Then there was a lull, during which, like the echo of the tempest, the dull and distant booming of the sea was borne to the affrighted listener's ears...Unable at length to control her feelings, grandmother got up out of her chair and went to the window, put aside the curtain and looked out...All at once she drew back with a low cry, saying in a broken voice: 'My God, father, it's Tom in his coffin! They're bringing him up here, to the house.' She then covered her face with her hands to shut out the horrid sight...No one could convince grandmother that she had not actually seen, with her own eyes, her dear boy Tom, the idol of her heart, lying cold in death. To her it was indeed a revelation from the tomb, for the ship in which Tom had sailed was never heard from again."*

Only a few months after this premonition of death there came another, at Eastport, Maine, to Irish-born Nora Breen. Her husband Bob, originally from Lubec, was captain of a ship he'd built himself, named NORA, sailing with cargo from port to port along the New England coast. Coming from Portland, the NORA was overdue, and the wife of her captain slept fitfully. Deep into the night, she was startled awake by the figure of a man standing by her bed. It was her husband, dripping wet and covered in seaweed. Nora screamed and, with trembling hands, lit her bedside lamp. The vision was gone, and at that moment she heard the clock in the Eastport church tower strike 1:00 a.m. As she leapt from her bed in terror, she noticed a puddle of water on the floor close by, and a string of kelp seaweed there with it. She cried for help, and others in the house came running. She told them what she had seen and showed them the puddle and seaweed. Her child actually tasted the water and found it salty. The seaweed she gathered up and placed in a box under the bed. Nora was frightened and considered this a terrible omen, but family and neighbors thought it just a figment of her active Irish imagination, especially as late the next morning the NORA was spotted on the horizon, coming safely into port. When she arrived, however, the crew had horrifying news—Captain Bob Breen had been struck by lightning as he stood at the helm in the dead of night, and had been lifted from the deck by the jolt and lost overboard. By the crew's report, it had happened at the same time Nora had her vision. She lived a widow for many years in Eastport, the seaweed wrapped in Irish lace in the box beneath her bed. Coincidentally, she died on the anniversary of the night her husband was lost at sea—or maybe it wasn't coincidence?

Nora Breen, it was said, was born with a veil or "caul," as they called it in the old country. As with others in bygone days who came out of the womb wearing this thin membrane of skin over their heads like a hood, she was considered blessed and credited with supernatural powers. In the village of Kilronan, where Nora was raised, the people were keenly superstitious; like the seaweed she carefully preserved at her husband's death, her caul would have also been preserved in a container and placed in a safe place within her Irish home. As Webster tells us, *"the caul, or hallihoo (holy hood), was thought by the super-stitious to bring good luck."* Although the caul was traditionally kept in the home as a kind of talisman, it was sometimes sold to sea captains at a good price, to protect ships from sinking and sailors from drowning. It was said that those born with a caul *"would never drown, could see ghosts, and could fore-see future events,"*—or so thought those of Celtic ancestry, mainly the Scots, Irish, Welsh, and Britons. The Italians and Spanish, who from Roman times also thought a caul contained magical powers, believed that bearers of the caul could predict tragedies and disasters, and therefore considered it an evil omen.

I, like Nora, was born with a caul, or so I am told, and perhaps this explains why I was able to predict my family home of the future when I was a teenager, just as it may explain Nora's vision of her dead husband by her bedside. What other reason could there be?

Captain Richard Brown of Cardiff, Wales, would never leave port for an Atlantic crossing without a caul neatly tucked into the top drawer of his cabin bureau. Before sailing on the USK, carrying coal and miscellaneous cargo, to the port of Huancho, Peru, in February of 1863, he traded a fine ship's compass to a fellow commander for the caul he had carried on his ship, which had just returned safely from the Americas. All went well aboard the USK until she reached the West Indies. Standing on deck alone at the helm, while the crew breakfasted below, Captain Brown had a strange, tingly sensation come over him and experienced a vision. It was of a woman in white, wearing a sheer veil which covered her face and head, standing before him. *"Go back from where you came,"* she said in a quivering, soft voice, *"and waste little time in doing so, for otherwise you will lose your vessel, your men, and yourself, and tell your employer that I ordained it."* The woman then vanished before his eyes. The shocked and bewildered captain called his men on deck, and ordered the USK back to Cardiff. The men followed his orders without question, but the first mate was perplexed and demanded an explanation for turning back. *"I have been given explicit instructions to turn back to home port,"* said Captain Brown without elaborating—but he had much explaining to do once he faced the ship and cargo owners in Wales. They thought his reason was senseless lunacy, and had him arrested for dereliction of duty. He was taken to trial in July, where his testimony was recorded and he was declared unfit for command of any and all vessels. He was allowed to retrieve all his possessions from the USK, including the caul, and was reduced to laboring in and around the docks. He watched the USK leave port that summer under a new commander, with the same cargo but not all the original crew. Some of them, after hearing Captain Brown's testimony at trial, refused to reboard the USK. Six months later, Brown's captains' papers were returned to him, and his previous employers begged him to return to work commanding a ship for them. Why the change of heart?—four months after sailing out of Bristol Channel, fire broke out aboard the USK while she was off the coast of Chile. The USK, her captain, and all her crew were burned to death at sea.

Another vision of a woman in white wearing a veil was reported eight years later in America's foremost fishing port of Gloucester, Massachusetts. A cook aboard the fishing schooner SACHEM, noted for his visions and second sight, approached the captain of the vessel while out fishing and begged him to return the ship to port. Captain Wenzell reported the incident in his logbook: *"September 7, 1871—Cook Nelson requested an urgent audience with me. He seemed agitated and fearful. He said he had just been awakened by a recurring dream. He said that the same dream had disturbed him twice before in his life, but what really rattled him was that on each of the two previous occasions it was followed by shipwrecks, tragedy, and death. As he spoke, he kept glancing around my cabin as though he feared eavesdroppers..."*

Nelson told the captain that, in his vivid dream, he saw a group of women of various ages, all dressed in white, waiting at a dock in a rainstorm. *"They were waiting for their men to return from a voyage,"* said Nelson, *"but the men never returned."* Nelson took it as a *"forerunner,"* a warning of disaster, and begged the captain to turn the ship around and head back to Gloucester before it was too late. Captain Wenzell, a disbeliever in such forewarnings, considered Nelson's dream *"superstitious nonsense,"* but the more he tried to calm his cook from his fears, the more emphatic Nelson became. Wenzell wasn't about to turn back; he had been sailing SACHEM for over two days, and was approaching the lush fishing grounds of George's Bank.

That evening, while anchored at the Banks, the weather turned bad, and as the schooner rocked and swayed in the giant swells, she sprung a leak. Water was filling the vessel so fast that the pumps couldn't handle the flow. Just as the captain and crew were about to abandon ship, another Gloucester schooner, PESCADOR, happened by. In the dead of night, during the raging storm, the PESCADOR captain and crew managed to maneuver their vessel close enough to the SACHEM so that Wenzell and his men could jump aboard, scant moments before their schooner sank under the waves. Cook Nelson's premonition of disaster had manifested for the third time in his life, and Captain Wenzell became a believer.

Three female spirits in white caused great consternation in the port village of Charlottetown, Prince Edward Island, on the morning of October 7, 1853. Alarm was sounded through the town when the great clanging bell of Saint James' belltower pealed out five distinct rings. People rushed to the church to see who was ringing the bell and for what reason. The doors were locked shut, but shortly after the fifth toll they were suddenly flung open, and there before the onlookers stood three women, all dressed in white. No one dared enter the church, for this was obviously a vision, and a few fell to their knees on the church steps. Three ghostly figures stood silently until the bell tolled twice more, then the doors slammed shut again, as if by a great gust of wind, and when they were tried again, they were locked. Peeking through a side window, two Charlottetown boys shouted to the crowd that they could see one of the women in white climbing the stairs to the belfry. The church minister then arrived with his keys and opened the doors. Four of the more courageous onlookers entered the church with the minister to search for these women, who some thought were holy spirits, while others concluded that they were only intruders intent on causing havoc. As the men headed up the stairs to the belfry, the bell tolled again, for the eighth time—but when they arrived in the steeple, the bell was silent and the bell rope securely tied. There was no sign of the women anywhere. Word of the vision of the three women in white spread through the town like wildfire, causing no end of gossip—but what did it mean, and why did the church bell strike eight times?

Though there was much speculation, there seemed to be no answer, until 8:00 a.m. the next morning, when Allen Cameron drifted ashore on the wheelhouse of a wrecked ship. He was all but frozen to death, and so exposed to the elements after drifting with the currents for six hours that he could not speak. Cameron had been a passenger aboard the steamer FAIRY QUEEN, which cruised between Charlottetown and Pictou, Nova Scotia, a voyage of only a few hours. She had hit high winds and sea, and at the same time sprung a leak that slowly filled the ship with water. Realizing that his ship was doomed, Captain Bulyea and most of his crew launched a lifeboat, leaving twenty passengers to fend for themselves on the listing steamer. At 2:00 a.m., the FAIRY QUEEN turned turtle, dumping all the passengers into the raging sea. Only twelve reached shore, hanging on to pieces of wreckage. Survivor Allen Cameron, once revived and able to speak, sobbed out just one sentence: *"I saw three women drown before my eyes, and I was unable to help them."* Were these the three women in white who rang the bell in the church, the villagers wondered? Although the answer will never be known, is it coincidence that the bell had tolled eight times, and that eight of the twenty passengers were drowned? The haunting warning had come before the steamer left port in Charlottetown, but there was no way of connecting the apparition with the FAIRY QUEEN. Captain Bulyea and his crew did arrive safely to shore in the lifeboat, and he was tried and convicted of dereliction of duty.

Almost a year later, on September 20, 1854, the 284–foot luxury steamer ARCTIC left Liverpool Harbor to cross the North Atlantic to New York, carrying 390 people aboard. On the day of her departure, one person on the passenger list, Caroline Mitchell, suddenly refused to sail on the ARCTIC. She and her brother Charles had been vacationing in London, and he was anxious to return home to his family in South Carolina. They had booked passage aboard the ARCTIC, but Caroline refused to go. The night before, she had a premonition that she would drown in a sea of fog, and so real was her vision that she considered it a true warning. Her brother couldn't believe she would change her plans just because of a bad dream, and he decided to leave her in Liverpool and join the passengers on the ARCTIC as he'd planned.

Seven days later, the swift steamer was at the Grand Banks, just three days from docking in New York. There was a slight fog, but as the ARCTIC commander, Captain James Luce, informed his helmsman, *"It is not foggy enough to station a lookout in the forecastle."* A few minutes later there was a crash at the bow, and the great ship shuddered. *"The bow of the strange ship that hit us appeared to be cut off for about ten feet,"* Captain Luce later reported. *"Seeing that in all probability she must sink in a few minutes, after taking a hasty glance at our own ship and believing that we were comparatively uninjured, my first impulse was to try to save the lives of those aboard the stranger. I immediately ordered two of our lifeboats lowered. It was after they were lowered that I was informed that the ARCTIC herself was in serious trouble."*

The *"strange ship,"* as Captain Luce described her, was the 200-ton steamer VESTA, with 197 crew and French fishermen on board, heading to France from Miquelon Island. Her commander also lowered two lifeboats, thinking his steamer would sink immediately. Carrying twelve men, one of the lifeboats headed for the ARCTIC, and what they hoped was safety; but they rowed too close to ARCTIC's paddlewheel. The lifeboat and eleven of its occupants were smashed to pieces by the wheel, and only one man was saved and hauled aboard the ARCTIC. Tragic as the accident was, Captain Luce took no time to retrieve bodies. He headed his bow toward Cape Race, Newfoundland, which was the closest land, over fifty miles away. While crewmen attempted to plug the leak in the ARCTIC's bow and side, filling the holes with mattresses, the steamer made a mad dash through the thickening fog. The ARCTIC lifeboats were lost in the fog, as was the sinking steamer VESTA. The VESTA crew, however, also using mattresses to plug her leaks, and with pumps going full tilt, managed to limp all the way to Newfoundland and safety. The only lives lost from the VESTA were those crushed under the ARCTIC paddlewheel.

Seawater was constantly rising in the hold of the ARCTIC, until it finally reached her boilers and the steam fires sizzled out, stopping the paddlewheel. The ARCTIC was dead in the water, surrounded by fog and buffeted by rough seas—she was doomed. Panic gripped the passengers and crew, who raced to launch the few lifeboats left hanging in the davits. In their haste, two of the boats spilled their occupants into the frigid sea, most of whom were never seen again. Amongst these unfortunates were Mrs. Collins and her two children, the family of the owner of the steamship line that operated the ARCTIC. In an attempt to save some of the other women and children, Captain Luce had a liferaft quickly built from the timbers of the pilothouse. Over seventy-five people boarded the makeshift raft before it was set adrift. Twenty-six long hours later, only one man stepped ashore, Peter McCabe of New York: *"One by one I saw my unfortunate companions drop off the raft,"* he reported, *"most from sheer exhaustion; some of them floated off and were eaten and gnawed by fishes..."*

George Burns, another passenger aboard the ill-fated ARCTIC, later reported that, *"At five that afternoon, her bow rose in the air and she began her plunge into the sea stern-first. There was one fearful shriek, but the most terrible noise of all, which drowned out all other sounds, was the ship's own death moans...an all but human-sounding wail, awful to hear."* Captain Luce went down with his ship, but managed to fight the waves while holding on to his eight-year-old son, whom he had brought along on the voyage to restore his failing health. When later rescued, Captain Luce said, *"A most awful and heart-rending scene presented itself to my view; women and children struggling together amidst pieces of wreckage of every kind, calling on each other and God to assist them...I was in the act of trying to save my child when a portion of the paddlebox came crashing up edgewise, grazing my head, and then it fell with its whole weight on the head of my darling child. In another moment I beheld him a lifeless corpse on the surface of the waves."*

Charles Mitchell later reflected that, as the ARCTIC was sinking, his first thought was not of his own survival, but a feeling of relief that his sister Caroline was not with him. Her premonition of disaster was indeed coming true before his very eyes: *"I reached for the ship's railing and grabbed a rope, by which I lowered myself and then jumped the remaining distance into the sea. I was stunned by the fall, but the freezing water revived me. I feebly swam to a half empty lifeboat and was hauled aboard. A fog then enveloped us and we drifted away from the sinking ship. We had no means of determining direction and we drifted for about forty-five miles. We finally followed a seabird that was flying overhead and hours later landed at the small fishing village of Broad Cove, Newfoundland...I remained for a month in a fisherman's hut before I recovered sufficiently from exposure to leave and return to Charleston."*

In all, 322 persons aboard the ARCTIC died, most from drowning, but others from exposure in the lifeboats or from drinking saltwater to quench their thirst. Most of the survivors were crew members; a staggering percentage of passengers perished. Charles Mitchell never doubted his sister's dreams of premonition again. In a strange quirk of fate, Charles and Caroline's nieces drowned twenty-four years later, while they were passengers aboard the steamer CHAMPION, which collided with another ship off the cost of the Carolinas. An uncle also drowned while boarding a ship at Charleston in 1870. It is not recorded whether or not Caroline predicted these drowning disasters in her family, but it seems clear that the Mitchells of South Carolina should avoid sea voyages!

The skeptic may conclude that Caroline Mitchell's decision not to sail aboard the ARCTIC was merely *"woman's intuition,"* that all such forebodings are usually unjustified, and the feeling that something bad may happen in the future never amounts to anything. This may be true, considering all the times we think something is going to happen and it doesn't; however, I personally believe, without doubt, that there is either a force—or perhaps some genetic quirk—that, under certain conditions and circumstances, provides a warning of impending tragedy. Also, as was my experience, it occasionally presents a pleasing prediction of future events. While we may never know what causes premonitions, if you ever seem to get an advance warning of things to come, I suggest you react as Caroline Mitchell did—no matter what the cost or inconvenience, heed your premonition.

The Dutch ship HERMANIA was found abandoned off the coast of England in 1849. The figurehead of a woman from the American vessel she collided with was wedged into the HERMANIA's wheelhouse, but both crews and the American ship vanished.

The stately five-masted schooner CARROLL A. DEERING is launched in 1919 at Bath, Maine, and is abandoned two years later at Oracoke Island, North Carolina, her captain and crew never being heard from again.

Captain Willis Wormell of the CARROLL A. DEERING, and the remains of the DEERING on the beach at Oracoke, before a hurricane smashed her into splintered timbers.
Photo courtesy of the North Carolina News Bureau.

VII
NOT A CLUE, NOR A CREW

They have cruised the ocean waves since well before Columbus, and continue to do so, often under tattered sail or still under steam, heading on no charted course, wandering aimlessly before the wind and currents of the wide Atlantic. They are sometimes spotted from land or a passing ship in one location, and years later in another. They are the derelicts of the sea, abandoned ships, left by captain and crew for a variety of reasons: fire aboard that rages out of control, rising water in the hold that threatens to sink the ship, a wild storm that so rattles the ship's timbers that the crew opts for an open boat rather than have the ship break apart under their feet. Then there are other, more bizarre reasons: a foul-smelling cargo forces captain and crew over the side, or a dangerous cargo threatens to explode; pirates invade the ship, killing or capturing her occupants before setting the ship adrift. It is not rare for a captain and crew to purposely abandon ship, believing she is about to sink at any moment, only to have that ship sail on indefinitely for weeks, months, even years.

The schooner GOVERNOR PARR, while sailing off Newfoundland in September, 1923, was swamped in a heavy gale. Her crew immediately abandoned her in longboats, believing she would sink at any moment. They were soon picked up by a passing ship, some 300 miles off shore. Four weeks later, the ship SAXONIA spotted the GOVERNOR PARR slowly drifting to Europe. The SAXONIA crew boarded her and found her in good condition, but for the fact that she was half filled with seawater. They left her and sailed on. The derelict schooner was spotted six more times within the next eight weeks. She now was sailing south. In late December, the cutter TAMPA was sent to sea to find her and tow her in, which she did; but, nearing port, TAMPA was low on fuel and had to cut the PARR loose to make port safely herself. The PARR was seen again six months later, sailing south, by passengers and crew aboard the steamer GLEN. It was reported that, *"the bowsprit and deckhouse were still intact, and she seemed quite seaworthy."* In July of 1924 she was spotted off the Canary Islands, and on August 8, a British liner lookout spied her again, this time off Africa. The captain of the liner considered her a *"nuisance to navigation,"* so he stopped his ship long enough to have his crew set the derelict afire. They watched her drift on ablaze, thinking surely she would burn to the waterline and soon sink, but the unsinkable GOVERNOR PARR sailed on. On August 11, she was spotted *"smoldering and barely afloat,"* by the crew of the ship UMTALI, and four days later was reported in the same condition by those aboard the IBERIA, but she hasn't been seen again since—which, of course, doesn't mean that she isn't still out there.

The steamer DUNMORE, carrying a heavy load of coal, was battered by a storm in the North Atlantic which set her rolling fretfully. The crew panicked

and abandoned her in mid-ocean on the night of January 19, 1906. The crew
was rescued and, at a hearing a few weeks later, the captain said he believed
the DUNMORE was about to sink when they left her, and that although he did-
n't see her go down, he was sure she sank shortly after he and his crew had
abandoned her—but she didn't. Within the following five weeks, the DUN-
MORE was sighted by at least sixteen ships. She was heading south, and one
steamer, the SAINT LOUIS, barely missed colliding with her in the dead of
night. The DUNMORE was located a month later off the Bahamas. American
gunboats were sent out to *"seek and destroy,"* which they did; after many shots
to her hull, the DUNMORE sank.

On a Sunday in November, 1901, the merchant ship ERIN'S ISLE came upon
a large sailing ship without masts, cruising slowly in the mid-Atlantic. Charles
Dixon, chief officer aboard the merchantman, decided to come alongside the
derelict and inspect her. His diary relates his experience: *"There was no sign of
life aboard her, and we wondered what had become of the crew? Had they been
killed in the disaster which had befallen the ship? Had they left in boats or
been taken aboard by a passing vessel, or were they still on board?...It could
easily be seen that she was an iron vessel and had been but recently in dock, as
the paint on her hull was fresh and clean...So, a boat was put out, and three
men and myself jumped into her and we left our ship. About a quarter to five
we were up on the wreck. In passing under her stern we read the name NOR-
FOLK ISLAND of Glasgow. As we pulled around the lee side so that we could
get a view of the deck, it nearly took my breath away to see such a sight; the
other side had looked so promising, but she had been completely burnt
out...The fire had done its work only too well. There was not a vestige of wood-
work to be seen; nothing but bent and twisted iron beams, broken bulwarks,
and the remains of the shattered masts. In the bottom of the vessel was about
150 tons of coal and cinders still smoldering. In the forward part was water
about three or four feet deep...In the cabin I noticed a clock, with the hands
still attached and stopped at three o'clock...We then went along to where the
cook house had been, and here found that, owing to its being protected from
the direct heat of the burning cargo by an iron deck, nearly everything was
intact; that is, the stove and most of the cooking utensils. I then went down into
the after hold on the top of the smoldering coal, but it was rather too hot and
stifling to stay...I climbed pretty well all over the vessel to see if there was anything of value...and I secured the ship's bell as a memento of our visit.

While I was down in the hold of the vessel I tried to realize the sensations of
one left alone on a vessel in this state. I was out of sight of our own ship and
could not see the men who had come on board the wreck with me. There were
heavy clouds in the sky, which at that time of day made it very gloomy. Add to
this the mournful sound made by the uncontrolled rudder moving with the sea,
the washing backward and forward of the water in the hold, together with a*

peculiar moaning sound as of someone in agony, made by the remains of the masts moving slowly as the vessel rolled...there came over me a feeling of such despair and hopelessness as I never again wish to experience...At about seven p.m. we saw the last of the NORFOLK ISLAND. As she faded from our sight in the gathering mists of evening she presented a picture of such desolation that it left an impression to be long remembered..."

Probably the best-remembered derelict of the Atlantic was the JAMES CHESTER. She was encountered under sail far at sea (latitude 30° N., longitude 40° W.) by British merchantman MARATHON on February 28, 1855. John Thomas, first mate aboard the MARATHON, reported that *"she was a largish ship of some 1000-odd tons, and if it weren't for her riggings being in such a state of disorder, and that she kept yawing and sailing in such an erratic fashion, we would have passed her by."*

Instead, the captain hailed the vessel with his bull-horn, but received no response. He then sent out Thomas with two other men in the longboat to board her. Within a few minutes, they were standing on deck of the wayward barque. *"It was absolutely deserted,"* Thomas later reported, *"there was no answer to my shouts but the flapping of canvas sails and the wash of waves against the vessel's hull...There was some disorder on deck; ends of rope were lying about, coils of halyards were lifted off the pins and thrown down, some portions of the rigging were adrift, and her sails were flying loose; yet she seemed a snug enough ship, her decks were in good color, the paint fresh, the brasswork fairly bright, and she was flush fore and aft, while her binnacles, pump, capstan, skylights, and companions were in excellent order. She lacked nothing but her crew..."*

Keeping close to one another, Thomas led his men below decks, and except for the groaning of the rudder, no other sound greeted them. The cabins they found in wild disarray, *"furniture overturned and pushed about, chests open and clothes scattered,"* but the hammocks were in order and there were no signs of blood or violence. Thomas did, however, notice that the compass and ship's charts were missing. The cargo of wool and provisions was neat in the hold and seemingly intact, and on deck the longboats were in their davits. If the crew had mutinied, how did they leave the ship, and why would they do so if the JAMES CHESTER was seaworthy, which she seemed to be? If they were attacked by pirates, wouldn't there be signs of bloodshed, and wouldn't they have taken the cargo? Pirates, also, would not abandon a perfectly good sailing vessel, but would have commandeered her for their own use.

The MARATHON took the JAMES CHESTER in tow and brought her into port, her captain claiming salvage rights of 60% of her value and of the cargo, which were the gong salvage rights at the time. The captain and crew of the derelict ship were never located; what caused them to abandon ship—if, indeed, that is what they did—remains a mystery.

Six years earlier, in 1849, another mystery ship, the HERMANIA, was discovered sailing aimlessly just a few miles off the English coast. John Hyde, fishing from his mackerel boat FAME, never would have taken a second glance at the 100-ton sailing vessel had she not fouled and tangled some of his nets as she sailed close by. Hyde hailed the ship without a response, and then he noticed that one of her masts was missing, broken clean off, leaving only a stump. Hyde decided to board her and, upon doing so, discovered that the foreign ship had received a crushing blow on her starboard side, amidships, which *"had carried away the bulwarks and probably caused her mast to crack."* Hyde and his crew then noticed that the figurehead of a woman was wedged into the roundhouse of the HERMANIA, along with gilding and some eight feet of another ship's bow—obviously from the ship she collided with. The two vessels, Hyde assumed, were interlocked; thinking the HERMANIA was about to sink, her crew leaped onto the ship that lost her figurehead. The HERMANIA, however, was watertight and not about to sink. Everything aboard her was in good order, and her longboats hung in the davits. All ropes aboard were neatly coiled, and below all cabins were neat. One cabin contained a cradle and women's clothing, and there were many personal valuables aboard, including a gold watch that was still ticking, plus chests of silver, unopened. Strangely, Hyde also discovered a binnacle lamp still burning, but not a living soul aboard. With the help of a trawler, Hyde towed the HERMANIA to the nearest port, Sutton Pool. Authorities there took charge of the crewless ship and Hyde never saw a penny of salvage money. The HERMANIA was a Dutch ship, as reported by the press, and it was concluded that the figurehead came from an American ship—but from what ship, it was never determined. The HERMANIA passengers and crew were never heard from. It is most likely that the American ship they leaped upon, thinking the HERMANIA was about to sink, herself disappeared under the waves, but the United States' records do not reveal any such ship being lost at that time.

Possibly the strangest incident involving a crewless American ship discovered sailing aimlessly in the mid-Atlantic is that of the MARY CELESTE; her story is still discussed as a prominent sea mystery. She was a two-masted brig, 282-tons and 98 feet long, carrying a cargo of 1,700 barrels of raw alcohol. She left New York heading across the North Atlantic to Genoa on November 7, 1872. Aboard were Captain Benjamin Briggs of Wareham, Massachusetts, along with his wife Sarah and their two-year-old daughter Sophia, plus seven crewmen. This was Briggs' first command aboard the CELESTE. It was 29 days later that Captain Morehouse of the British barque DEI GRATIA, also out of New York, came upon the CELESTE sailing erratically off the AZORES, without a soul aboard her. The DEI GRATIA crew explored the CELESTE, and although there was some seawater below decks, she was seaworthy. In the main cabin they found women's clothing and toys scattered about, and the ship's log with the last entry dated November 25th. The forehatch cover was open, and the sextant and chronometer, plus the ship's longboat, were missing; otherwise, all was in order. Captain Morehouse ordered three of his crewmen to sail the CELESTE behind the DEI GRATIA into Gibraltar, where the captain claimed salvage rights. He received only $8,000 for his trouble, and was falsely accused of piracy on the high seas. To this day, nobody knows what happened to the ten people aboard the CELESTE; of the many theories, however, one that seems most plausible is that in the warmer climate as the ship approached Europe, increased temperatures could have caused expansion of the alcohol barrels and leakage. Smelling fumes, the cautious captain may have thought the alcohol was about to explode, placing everyone in the longboat to avoid catastrophe. The CELESTE then outsailed the longboat, and the overcrowded boat sank as they attempted to make the nearest land. All other theories of mutiny and piracy pale in comparison. The CELESTE, of course, was immediately considered a jinxed ship by superstitious sailors, and it was nearly impossible to obtain a crew to sail her. Extra pay was offered to crew her, and she did sail again, but wrecked off Haiti on January 3, 1885. Her owner and captain, however, were convicted in court of sinking her on purpose for the insurance money.

Perhaps an even greater odyssey concerns the schooner ELIZA ANN, which left Boston on December 11, 1832, and wasn't seen again for over a year. A fisherman out of Ely Harbor, Bermuda, came upon a derelict drifting in offshore currents. Her bow was partially submerged, and the smell from her was almost unbearable, but the fisherman boarded her to find the deck strewn with eight skeletons dressed in tattered clothes. With the help of fellow Bermudans, the derelict was towed into the shallows; hoping to find treasure, the salvagers entered her stinking hold only to find a cargo of fish, pork, butter, beef, cider, and brandy, all decaying except for the latter two items. British authorities, upon studying the skeletons and clothing, found the name "J. Seaver" sewn into one shirt, and a Ben Franklin silver medal on a chain around the bony neck of a skeleton. On it were inscribed the words, *"As a reward of merit to William Brown."* There had been two brothers named Seaver aboard the ELIZA ANN, and the ship was commanded by a James Brown, whose two cousins, one named William, were members of the crew. Since the ELIZA ANN had been heading for Guyana with a supply of foodstuffs, it was concluded that this derelict, discovered on December 27, 1833, was the ELIZA ANN. Like the MARY CELESTE, theories of what had happened to her abounded, both in Boston and Bermuda: wrecked in a storm, pirates, mutiny—but none make sense. The crew certainly didn't starve to death, or die of thirst, for their cargo would have supplied them for months, maybe years if properly preserved in brine or salt, both of which were available. There was no sign of wounds on the skeletons, so a sea battle or mutiny seems unlikely. An encounter with a vicious storm seems most likely, for her masts were cracked, but the ship remained afloat and the men died on deck. Why couldn't they have survived? We'll never know the answer to this sea mystery. One intriguing afterglow to the derelict ELIZA ANN is that her wood was used in the building of a house located near Ely Harbor, and that the house today is haunted by the periodic appearance of skeletons knocking at the front door.

As haunting as ELIZA ANN's mystery is, that of the SEABIRD of Newport, Rhode Island is even more puzzling. She was due in port from Honduras in October of 1750, but never arrived. Her owner, Isaac Steele, feared the worst; in mid-November, however, Steele was overjoyed to hear that his brig was spotted offshore and heading in. He rushed to the wharf and waited with the family and friends of her captain and crew, but the SEABIRD didn't sail into harbor, turning instead into Conrad's Cove, to a beach beyond the harbor mouth. Trouble with her rudder or steering mechanism, thought Steele. With an ever-increasing entourage, Steele raced for the beach in the hope of greeting his captain, John Huxham. The SEABIRD was undamaged, but neither Huxham nor any of the crew were there to greet Steele and the others. With the exception of a dog, the ship was empty—not a person aboard, yet the deck and all cabins were in good order. Isaac Steele was devastated, as were the other bystanders. Why had the captain and crew disappeared? Who but the crew would have steered the SEABIRD to the beach? And why not bring the ship into her berth at the wharf? To add to the mystery, three days later the SEABIRD herself was missing, gone from the beach, without anyone seeing her sail off. Isaac Steele, and the family and friends of the captain and crew of the Newport brig never heard from the original occupants of the SEABIRD, nor was the ship herself ever seen again.

As you consider the many perplexing scenarios of the whys and wherefores concerning the SEABIRD, I'll tell you of one last, mysterious derelict, whose story has confounded mariners and landlubbers alike for some seventy-seven years. Her rise to notoriety began one bright, calm evening on February 1, 1921, at the Cape Hatteras Coast Guard Station. A report came in from a fisherman that a large, beautiful white schooner, under full sail, was becalmed and seemingly stuck on Outer Diamond Shoal of Oracoke Island. A cutter was dispatched to investigate. At dawn, when the Coast Guardsmen sighted her, *"She was stuck fast on the sandshoal,"* reported the cutter helmsman, *"in a relatively calm sea. She was such an awesome sight that I had to look away and blink my eyes, then look back. She was a five-masted queen of the seas, one of the biggest and finest schooners I'd ever seen, with every canvas up to the topsail set, out to the furthermost jib..."* There was only a light breeze, but the grand ship was being driven harder aground toward shore by each wave. The cutter circled the schooner and hailed her, but there was no one on deck and no response to their calls. Unless invited aboard, or told by the captain or members of the crew that she was in distress, the Coast Guardsmen, by law, could not board her. Upon circling her again before returning to base, the cutter crew copied her name from the transom: CARROLL A. DEERING.

Back at the station, the keeper checked the naval register and found the DEERING, a fairly new schooner, was launched at Bath, Maine, on April 4, 1919. Her owner, Gardiner Deering, was notified by telegraph regarding the status of his vessel. He replied to the Coast Guard, asking that a boarding party be sent to determine what might be wrong, and to ascertain why captain and crew hadn't responded. The cutter returned to Diamond Shoal, and a crew of six seamen with an ensign boarded the DEERING, even though it was felt that she wasn't in deep trouble and probably could have easily slid off the sandy bottom without difficulty. Aboard, everything was in order. As one crewman commented, *"she looked like she had been prepared for inspection."* Every cabin was neat and clean, and the captain's liquor cabinet was untouched. It was noted, however, that all navigational instruments—sextant, telescope, quadrant, and charts—were missing, as was the schooner's logbook and long-boat. In the dining saloon, dinner was set out on the table, with food in each plate and coffee in the cups, but it didn't look as if anyone had taken a bite or a sip, and nothing was spilled. In the galley, food was cooking on the stove, but the fire had gone out and the food was lukewarm. The apprehensive and jittery Coast Guardsmen almost panicked when a moan came from behind the stove, and were much relieved when a fat calico cat greeted them. As they completed their inspection, the wind picked up and the seas began to chop, so they—like the crew before them, it seemed—abandoned the vessel and, with the cat in hand, returned to the station to report to the owner in Maine. Gardiner Deering concluded that either pirates had attacked his vessel, or the crew had mutinied, killing the captain and first mate and throwing them overboard before taking the longboat, setting themselves and the vessel adrift. But if it were pirates or a disgruntled crew, what happened to them? The U.S. Coast Guard, the Department of Commerce, the Justice Department, and the U.S. Army, conducted an immediate investigation of the surrounding sea and coast, lasting weeks and covering hundreds of square miles, but nothing was ever found, and there wasn't even a hint of pirates or mutineers. The captain, mate, and crew had simply disappeared into thin air, as if abruptly interrupted as they sat down for a hearty meal aboard the DEERING, without having time to take a single bite.

There had been ten men aboard the vessel when she left Portland, Maine, for Lewes, Delaware. En route, Captain William Merritt became extremely ill and was relieved of command by Captain Willis Wormell at Lewes. Wormell, an experienced commander of multi-masted vessels, sailed to Rio to unload his cargo of coal, then sailed on to Barbados in the West Indies. At Bridgetown, Barbados, authorities later learned that the crew was involved in a brawl. One crewmember named McLellan was jailed; after the captain paid for his release, the schooner sailed for the East Coast of America without a cargo. When the DEERING sailed past Frying Pan Lightship off the Carolinas on January 23, the lightship keeper reported that everything seemed in order aboard her. When she passed Cape Lookout Lightship six days later, the keeper there reported that "the crew was lolling about the deck," and that *"a redheaded man at her wheel hailed us, reporting that the DEERING had lost both her anchors in a storm, and he asked that other vessels give her a wide berth for that reason."* The redheaded man was probably Finlander Johan Frederickson, who was boatswain aboard the schooner. That was the last time the CARROLL A. DEERING was seen until she was reported stranded under full sail at Diamond Shoals, three days later.

The derelict schooner was so deeply embedded in the sand at Oracoke Island that she couldn't be salvaged, but whatever was of value aboard her was brought ashore. She slowly nudged closer to the land over the years, until islanders living along the shore petitioned the government to destroy her. Their complaint wasn't of the decaying hulk herself, but that birds, mostly gulls, lived on the wreck at night, constantly crying, squawking, and mewing like the hideous and mournful cries of humans in distress. It was a haunting sound which frightened the children and disturbed many an islander's sleep. The Coast Guard set out with guns loaded and explosives aboard to destroy the DEERING, but hurricane-force winds prevented them from going to sea. On that very evening, the DEERING broke to pieces in the storm, and scattered the timbers of her hull up and down the beach. The frightening sounds from the CARROLL A. DEERING are no longer heard, but the silence of her timbers along the beach still provide a chilling reminder of those who disappeared so mysteriously aboard one of the most regal ships that ever sailed the North Atlantic.

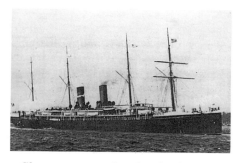 

She was reputed to be the fastest and most luxurious ship afloat, until July 4, 1898. That day, she acquired a most evil reputation. The French passenger liner LA BOURGOGNE, after colliding with the CROMAR-TYSHIRE off Nova Scotia, became "a ship of horror with a crew of monsters," said one survivor. Of her 570 passengers, only 65 survived, but most of her cowardly crew lived.

VIII
ETERNAL PHANTOMS

"Four A.M.—the FLYING DUTCHMAN crossed our bow. She emitted a strange phosphorescent light as of a phantom ship all aglow, in the midst of which light the masts, spars and sails of a brig 200 yards distant stood out in strong relief as she came up on the port bow where also the officer of the watch from the bridge saw her, as did also the quarter-deck midshipman, who was sent forward at once to the forecastle, but on arriving there was no vestige nor any sign whatever of any material ship to be seen either near or right away to the horizon, the night being clear and the sea calm."

This was the official entry in the log of the H.M.S. INCONSTANT, a major fighting ship of the British Navy, on July 11, 1881, signed by thirteen naval officers. Among those who testified to seeing the FLYING DUTCHMAN phantom ship was a young prince, later known as George V, King of Great Britain. If a king can swear to seeing such a unique phenomenon, perhaps we should reconsider our rejection of ancient tales and legends of such sightings from superstitious mariners, and from our own Puritanical forefathers when this nation was in her infancy. The legend of the FLYING DUTCHMAN is hundreds of years old, but the belief by seamen that she really existed lasted well into the eighteenth century. Today, we usually consider phantom ships akin to mermaid sightings and leprechaun encounters, yet there are those living in the Maritimes and upper Maine who cling to the belief that these ghostly vessels do exist. We must consider, too, that the sightings of phantom ships has not subsided, and that they are most prevalent in the North Atlantic.

Helen Creighton, Canadian historian, tells us that only a few years back, *"Some Tancook men were on the Banks off Newfoundland one night when they saw a ship bearing down on them with masthead lights showing. She was full-rigged and had all the lights on she was required to carry, and no more and no less. The captain and his watchman stood uncertainly as she approached, waiting to see what she would do. They were tacking at the time and the ship passed them like a ball of fire. They knew that this was no friendly gesture, but that they had seen a ghost ship. they feared it was a forerunner of disaster and they were nervous until they got back to their home port."*

From the southern end of the North Atlantic comes a similar story by another Canadian, navigator Hadley Doty of the cable-laying ship CYRUS FIELD, some twenty miles off the Carolinas. *"It was a clear night,"* he reported in May of 1946. *"All of a sudden a lookout yelled, 'Hard over!', meaning the ship should change course as quick as possible. The watch saw a square-rigged sailing ship cut across our bow. They couldn't see anyone on her but there was a light in the captain's cabin, aft. The course alteration was noted in the log and reported to the Coast Guard in New York. The Coast Guard told us there had been several similar incidents that night...The Phantom ship came out of nowhere and seemed to disappear just as quickly."*

A few years ago, Bill Prosser, aboard the 85–foot underwater research vessel UNDERSEA HUNTER, off Florida, reported that, *"a glowing illumination"* off the starboard bow momentarily blinded him. It was a large ship, yet it didn't show on his radar screen. *"It looked like a huge resort hotel of several levels,"* he reported, and she was *"running a parallel course with the UNDERSEA HUNTER."* As Prosser wrestled with the wheel to avoid colliding with this phantom ship, *"it moved forty-five degrees in a matter of seconds, then vanished as quickly as it appeared,"* he said, *"and there wasn't another vessel in sight."* The apparition frightened Bill Prosser; he called it his *"FLYING DUTCHMAN-HILTON."*

No one knows if there was once a real vessel named FLYING DUTCHMAN that spawned the legend. Authorities on the subject have, over the years, generally concluded that the skipper of the DUTCHMAN was a thirteenth-century nobleman who murdered his wife and his own brother, whom he thought were lovers, only later discovering that they were not. The torture of his mistake drove him to sail the seas forever in a wild rage, daring each tempest to destroy him and his vessel, but to no avail—he sails on. Another variation is that a Dutchman named Bernard Fokke made a pact with the devil, so that his vessel could be the fastest in the world. To gain the man's soul, the devil agreed; but instead of one lifetime, Fokke was obliged to swiftly sail the seven seas forever. Over the centuries, thousands of sailors have returned to home port after long voyages to tell their friends and families that they had seen the dreaded FLYING DUTCHMAN. Many who saw it considered the vision bad luck, both for themselves and the ship they sailed in, so we must presume that many who saw it never returned home to tell their family and friends.

Imagine the audacity of a clippership owner naming his vessel FLYING DUTCHMAN. She was launched in 1852, one of the fastest clippers to make the run from New York to San Francisco. Her name, however, soon overpowered her performance. Inexplicable events began to occur aboard— accidents, broken engine parts, torn sails, etc.—and she began to slow down for no apparent reason. On her way home to New York in October 1857, after a rough voyage around Cape Horn, she passed the ship STARLIGHT in the Atlantic. The STARLIGHT commander said she *"seemed in good order and was sailing swiftly north,"* but the FLYING DUTCHMAN never made it back to home port. For some unknown reason, she hit Brigantine Beach, New Jersey, and wrecked, with most of her occupants saved but the ship a complete loss. The clipper FLYING DUTCHMAN had lived up to her name and, to my knowledge, no other ship owner was fool enough to name his vessel after this phantom of the sea.

In my home town of Salem, Massachusetts, before the witch hysteria, the pious Puritans were also haunted by a phantom ship, although I must confess there have been no sightings of it off the coast in my lifetime. They believed as much in the Devil existing on earth and working his evil ways as they did in God and His wonders. So it is no wonder that they believed that Captain Mark Walford, commander of the NOAH'S DOVE, was the Devil himself, even though his vessel was given a benevolent biblical name. Their negative feelings towards Walford probably were due to his looks—he was an ugly man, with pop-eyes and buck teeth—and to his attitude, for he was a gruff, grumbling, daring seafarer. It was 1676, and the Great Indian War of New England was over, allowing the men to continue uninterrupted trade with Europe and Canada. The NOAH'S DOVE was scheduled to sail for England, with a full cargo of goods and passengers, including a newly married couple, Mr. and Mrs. Walter Severn. The locals, including the Puritan minister, begged them not to sail with Captain Walford, whom they considered the *"Devil incarnate,"* but the Severns wanted quick passage from savages and wild country to civilized society. It was a Friday and stormy—two bad omens for a day of departure, thought the Puritans—but Captain Walford was determined to sail, and if the Severns wanted to get to their beloved England, they must leave with him. Before the ship lifted anchor, a large crow landed on the top of the mainmast and continued to caw loudly as the passengers boarded—another ominous warning, thought the Salemites. They begged friends and loved ones not to sail on NOAH'S DOVE, but all warnings went unheeded. Captain Walford, with a sneer for those at dockside, headed his vessel out into the Atlantic, and she was never seen nor heard from again—at least not in physical form. The Puritan leader of the day, Reverend Cotton Mather, writes in his book <u>Magnalia Christi</u> that, *"four days after a great gale, a ship was seen coming up Salem Bay. All rushed to the shore to witness the spectacle—a large vessel, covered with canvas from deck to truck...She sailed in the very wind's eye, with all her sails full as if sailing with a fair breeze...Suddenly, a stream of fire ran down the mainmast, then a cloud of smoke arose, the sails disappeared, yards, rigging and spars melted and the hull sank, leaving the surface of the Bay clear and smiling..."* This, the spectators recognized, was the NOAH'S DOVE, returning home as a spectre-ship, to notify them that all their friends and relatives had perished aboard her. The Devil, Captain Walford, had done his evil deed. This phantom was sighted periodically throughout the seventeenth century in and around Salem's outer harbor, *"a spiritual rover,"* Mather called it, and those who saw it close up, usually on foggy days, saw a man and woman on board, presumably the frightened newlyweds, Walter Severn and his pretty wife. Most reported that the phantom was sailing backwards. We must remember, however, that sixteen years later, in 1692, the backward sailing phantom was replaced by sightings of witches flying on broomsticks.

Cotton Mather also recorded another phantom ship that nearly devastated the seaside town of New Haven, Connecticut, in 1647. Governor John Winthrop of the Bay Colony also wrote of it in his Journal. The town fathers of New Haven, hoping to begin a lucrative business of trade with England, had a ship built for that purpose in neighboring Rhode Island. When the ship was delivered, her designated skipper, Captain Lamberton, was not satisfied with the vessel. He called her *"lopsided and cranky,"* but the owners were anxious to get started, so she was loaded with lumber, hides, furs, peas, and a small fortune in silver plate donated from the cupboards of townies to purchase needed supplies from England. Lamberton was reluctantly persuaded to sail the new ship, named the FELLOWSHIP, and the entire population of the town, less those who were passengers aboard, was at the dock to send her off with cheers and prayers for a good voyage. Their fortunes and futures were aboard the FELLOWSHIP as she sailed down Connecticut's Thames and out of sight. Governor Winthrop also reminds us that the passengers, too, *"were of very precious account."* An entire year went by without word from the FELLOWSHIP. Other ships arrived at New Haven from England without hearing any word about the town's own ship. Fearing the worst, a day of prayer was set aside on the anniversary of the FELLOWSHIP's sailing, and from the pulpit Reverend Davenport begged God to *"Let us hear what He has done with our dear friends."* The minister's prayers were answered, for as Cotton Mather tells us, *"there were eyewitnesses to this wonderful thing, and I venture to publish it for a thing as undoubted as it is wonderful."*

Six weeks after the day of prayer, on a sultry late afternoon just after a thunderstorm, the FELLOWSHIP came sailing up the river, but she was sailing in the sky and not on the water. One eyewitness to this spectacular scene was town father James Pierpont, and he writes of the incident as follows: *"She came with her canvas and colours abroad, though the wind be northernly, appeared in the air coming up from our harbour's mouth, which lyes southward from the town, seemingly with her sails filled under a fresh gale, holding her course north, and continuing under observation sailing against the wind for the space of half an hour. Many were drawn to behold this great work of God; yea, the very children cryed out, 'There's a brave ship!' At length crouding up as far as there is usually water sufficient for such a vessel, and so near some of the spectators, as they imagined a man might hurl a stone on board her, her maintop seemed to be blown off, but left hanging in the shrouds; then her missentop; then all her masting seemed blown away by the board: quickly after the hulk brought unto a careen, she overset, and so vanished into a smoaky cloud, which in some time dissipated, leaving, as every where else, clean air. The admiring spectators could distinguish the several colours of each part, the principal rigging, and such proportions, as caused not only the generality of persons to say, 'This was the mould of their ship, and this was the tragick end'*

but also Mr. Davenport in publick declared to this effect: 'That God had conde-
scended, for the quieting of their afflicted spirits, this extraordinary account of
his sovereign disposal of those for whom so many fervent prays were made
continually.'"

Probably the most popular phantom ship in the northeast is the PALATINE of
Block Island, off the coast of Rhode Island. This ghostly burning ship has been
seen by islanders and mainlanders continuously for over 250 years. The real
ship PALATINE had a gruesome history. She was sailing from Palatinates to
Philadelphia, in the autumn of 1752, loaded down with 340 German and Dutch
emigrants and a motley crew. Halfway across the Atlantic, the captain of the
PALATINE died, possibly murdered, and his body was dumped overboard.
Without leadership or discipline, the crew mutinied and began harassing the
passengers, stealing their few possessions and withholding food supplies from
them. The crew then deserted the ship, leaving the passengers without food,
water, or longboats. They were all helpless, not one among them knowing how
to sail or direct the ship. The PALATINE drifted aimlessly, her passengers
slowly dying of thirst or hunger. Two days after Christmas, she struck Sandy
Point, Block Island, and stranded there, her passengers too weak to swim the
few feet to shore. The islanders, however, considered the PALATINE a late
Christmas present, for many living there were wreckers. Imagine their disap-
pointment when they found the grand ship devoid of all riches, already
absconded by the thieving crew, and the deck and cabins littered with sick and
diseased passengers. The history becomes clouded at this point, and is debated
to this day, as to whether the islanders assisted and cared for the half-dead passengers or concentrated on saving the ship as salvage. It is agreed, however,
that a new tide and a shifting wind took the vessel back out to sea with one
passenger still aboard, a poor, demented woman, who some say carried a child,
and that the ship caught fire. The cries of the crazed woman filled the air as the
PALATINE drifted off, completely consumed by fire, until she sank. She
returns, usually in November and December, as a phantom ship, still ablaze,
and sometimes the spectre of a frantic woman holding an infant is seen running
up and down the deck in horrified panic.

"This curious irradiation rises from the ocean near the northern point of the
island," wrote islander Dr. Aaron Willy in 1811. *"Its appearance is nothing*
different from a blaze of fire. Whether it actually touches the water, or merely
hovers over it, is uncertain...At times it expands to the highness of a ship with
all her canvas spread, mostly in calm weather which precedes an easterly or
southerly storm. ...I first saw it in 1810. It was large and gently lambent, very
bright, broad on the bottom and terminating acutely upward...It continued
about fifteen minutes from the time I first observed it...This lucid meteor has
long been known as the Palatine Light. By the ignorant and superstitious it is
thought to be supernatural..."

Around the same time as Doctor Willy's testimony, farmer Ben Cogdon, living on the mainland at Charlestown, Rhode Island, wrote in his Journal of the phantom ship, *"I have seen her eight or ten times, and in those early days nobody doubted her being sent by an Almighty power...We lived, when I was young, directly opposite Block Island, where we used to have a plain view of the burning ship..."* In the 1880s, Rowland Robinson writes of his two friends, Shedrick Card and George Sheffield, *"two venerable old patriarchs, both of whom were very intelligent, that neither had the least doubt of their having seen the ship all in flames. Her bona-fide appearance was no more than an ordinary occurrence."* Robinson, in his <u>Recollections Of Olden Times</u>, also wrote that, *"there was an old man living on Block Island that always became madly insane after Christmas, and would rave about seeing a ship all ablaze, with men falling from her burning rigging and shrouds."*

It wasn't just in olden times that the phantom ship was seen. Only a few years ago, islander Annie Rose announced she had seen the PALATINE *"eight or ten times, maybe more. The Almighty sends the ship,"* she says, *"to let us know that He hasn't forgotten the wickedness of the island wreckers."* Hotel manager Venetia Rountree says that, *"Most of the seven hundred plus people living on the island in winter have seen the PALATINE. My brother Sam saw it several times. I was walking home one night late in November, and I happened to glance out at the Sound and saw a flickering glow. The light grew bigger as it approached the shore, and then I recognized it. It was the old PALATINE, back to warn us of a storm."* Coast Guardsmen stationed on the island are constantly being called out by boaters and mainlanders who claim to have seen a ship burning at sea off the island. They are obliged to search, but claim they have never encountered a burning spectre ship. *"Probably natural phosphorescence,"* is the official explanation from the Coast Guard.

There are many other spots along the north Atlantic coast of America and Canada where phantom vessels are seen, but unlike the PALATINE, the names of these haunted vessels are often not known, nor their history. Most times these sailing ghosts are reported to be on fire, under full canvas, moving swiftly, and appear before or after storms. They've also been seen at times sailing in the clouds, or even over ice. Helen Creighton writes of a man from Spry Bay, Nova Scotia, living on the Bay at Mushaboom one winter, *"when the water froze over and there was a foot of ice over the Bay, he heard a noise. He looked up and saw a full-rigged ship coming across the ice. It was the fourth day of February."* In March of 1985, Carol Livingston and her sisters saw a phantom ship off the coast of Prince Edward Island, Canada. *"It was really eerie,"* she reported, *"and we at first thought it was the New Brunswick lights, but it was too close. It was a phantom ship, and we knew it couldn't be a real ship, because the Strait was frozen solid."*

Probably the most vivid description of a phantom ship was one that appeared in Charlottetown Harbor, Prince Edward Island, reported by local historian Sterling Ramsey in the early 1900s. There was a group of some twenty dock workers who first saw it, *"some distance out in the channel. It was what appeared to be a large three-masted sailing vessel which was ablaze from bow to stern. Her crew was seen frantically running from one side of the ship to the other in their efforts to quell the many blazes which ravaged the vessel."* The workers, led by John MacLean, alerted town authorities, for they at first thought the ship was truly a distressed vessel, and a rescue boat was sent out, filled with men trained in ship rescue procedures. Just before they arrived on the scene, the ship disappeared. Boats searched the area and divers were even sent below to probe the underwater area where she was last seen, but after the excitement subsided it was determined by all that they had seen a phantom ship. She has been seen in the harbor since, still on fire with the crew rushing about frantically to put out the flames. Skeptics would, of course, consider this a case of mass hallucination, and although all these stories and eyewitness reports of phantom ships may be difficult to fathom, we cannot discard them as pure fantasy either. As we debate their reality, these phantoms continue to sail on into eternity.

The twin sisters, OLYMPIC and TITANIC, at Belfast, Ireland. Both seemed cursed from their launchings and shared haunting histories.
Photo from the Ralph Whitney collection.

Two New York headlines, one on April 15, 1912, stating all were saved on the TITANIC; the other, a day later, pronouncing the true tragedy.

Bruce Ismay, Managing Director of the White Star Line, was considered a coward, for he left the sinking TITANIC in a lifeboat. Captain Smith (above) was considered by most to be a hero, mainly because he went down with the ship.
Photos courtesy of Underwood and Underwood, New York.

IX
HEROES AND COWARDS

"The Wreck of the Hesperus" was sold by its author, Henry Wadsworth Longfellow, that morning in New York City for $25.00. He was scheduled to return home on the 488–ton sidewheel steamer LEXINGTON later that same day, but he changed plans at the last minute. Longfellow later said he decided to stay in New York to lecture, but the East River was almost frozen over with below zero temperatures and snow was falling—bleak conditions for a boat ride—or perhaps it was a premonition that made Longfellow strike his name from the manifest. The LEXINGTON sailed without the famous poet that chilly day of January 13, 1840, her passengers and crew about to experience the nightmare of their lives, much akin to those who sailed on the fictitious HESPERUS.

Captain George Child feared the ice in the river and in Long Island Sound, for plowing through it could damage the 220–foot LEXINGTON's huge side-wheel paddles. He also was nervous about the heavy iron safe that was chained to the main deck, filled with $140,000 in silver coins and bars, to be delivered to Harnden's Express Company in Providence, Rhode Island, which was the steamer's destination. Aboard was Alophus Harnden, owner of the Express Company, and there were also five sea captains aboard, which Captain Child thought unusual, and 112 others, most returning home to New England after a long holiday in New York. Aside from the passengers, there was a 32–man crew, considered an obstinate lot by the captain, because they had delayed loading the cargo of cotton bales in New York, complaining that it was too cold to work. It was one of these crewmen, as the ship steamed off Norwalk, Connecticut, who noticed a crack at the base of the ship's smokestack that was blowing sparks onto the cotton bales. he notified the captain, but his discovery came too late—the cotton bales were on fire. An attempt was made to extinguish the flames with a bucket brigade, but the fire was soon out of control. Captain Child decided to race for the Long Island shore, rather than Connecticut, where he thought he might beach his burning ship, but the wind fanned the flames and the LEXINGTON quickly became an inferno. The crew and passengers panicked and they battled for the lifeboats, the burly crewmen winning. The steamer, however, was moving too fast to successfully lower the lifeboats, and each one in turn swamped, drowning all its occupants. Only two miles from shore, the fire ate through the rudder control assembly and the ship began drifting with the currents further and further from shore. *Mayhem broke out among the remaining crew,"* reported David Crowley, one of only four survivors of the disaster, *"and the captain and first mate disappeared from the bridge and deserted the steamer. The crew, without a commander, showed little or no regard for the welfare and safety of the passengers, and many passengers were pleading for help. Only the reflections of the flames offered a small visible indication that the yelling came from persons treading water in the blackened night..."*

Some passengers untied the few bales of cotton that had not yet caught fire and threw them over the side before jumping into the icy sea, climbing onto the bales and paddling them as best they could with frozen hands towards the shore. Two passengers, Ben Cox and Charleston Hilliard, *"paddled our raft toward the shoreline, but Cox, frozen by the icy water, could not continue. He went under without a sound,"* Hilliard testified at the court hearing. The flames could be seen from both coasts, and although rescue boats were sent out, none of them returned with survivors. The sloop IMPROVEMENT, under command of Captain William Terrelle, was only three miles away from the inferno, but the captain testified later that *"I dare not approach the burning vessel, for fear of losing the tide. I desperately needed a higher tide to clear a nearby sandbar."* As he waited, the LEXINGTON burned through her hull and sank, with only dead bodies remaining on the surface waters—147 of them, some drowned, others frozen, and still others burned to death. At the court hearing, Captain Terrelle was deemed a coward, but given no punishment. The missing Captain Child and his first mate were also declared cowards by the court, as was the LEXINGTON's entire crew. The owner of the vessel, which he called his "White Lady," was the wealthy Cornelius Vanderbilt. The Board of Inquiry found him at fault, and the tragedy itself *"an act of murder,"* but no one was fined or sent to prison. Although the wreck of the LEXINGTON was discovered some two miles off shore in fairly shallow water by diver Ray Wagner in 1952, and has been periodically explored by noted diver and writer Clive Cussler, the iron safe with the valuable silver in it has yet to be found—or so we're told.

There are many "ifs" connected with the loss of the LEXINGTON. If Longfellow had joined the passengers as he was supposed to, would he have been "murdered" too? His final, illustrous poem would have been, ironically, "The Wreck of the Hesperus." But most importantly, if the captain and crew had acted heroically, surely many more passengers would have lived. In fact, if they had just done their duty—slowed the ship so that they could properly lower the lifeboats, diminish the flames, maintain order, assist the panicked passengers, and not be first to leave the burning ship—it wouldn't have been such an overwhelming tragedy. Was it the combination of intense cold and heat that caused "mayhem" aboard? In such extremities, one wonders, how would we behave in similar circumstances? Would we be cowards or heroes, or would it depend on the circumstances? I feel very at home on or around the sea, and assume I would be self-disciplined in an emergency; I may even be a hero. However, in high places, above seven feet or so, I might panic. I have a great fear of heights, and should an emergency arise when my feet are not on the ground, I just might respond in a cowardly fashion. A person hanging from a ladder, for instance, who desperately needed my help, would probably hang there forever, without my lending a hand. We also must realize that mass hysteria is indeed contagious—if one man panics, most likely all will. And so, these "cowards," who turned a beautiful "White Lady" into a nightmarish ship of horrors, should not, perhaps, be so easily judged. Under different circumstances, they may have reacted with honor.

Almost thirty-two years later, another Long Island steamer experienced a fate similar to the LEXINGTON's. She was of the same size, 220–feet long, and also carried a cargo of cotton. It was late evening, November 21, 1871, and the CITY OF NEW LONDON had left New London, Connecticut, in a snow-squall after dropping off some fifty passengers, and headed towards her home port of Norwich with just seven passengers aboard. Steaming up the Thames, fog as well as snow hindered her progress, so Captain Bill Brown decided to anchor off Montville until visibility improved. While anchored, river pilot Ed Ewen noticed a glow aboard the steamer, coming from a ventilator. The captain investigated and discovered the kitchen on fire. Brown called out his fire-guard, and within minutes the flames were quelched—or so the captain thought. He weighed anchor and continued upriver. Behind the galley was where the cotton bales were stowed, and a spark from the charred kitchen wall started a slow burn of the cotton. As the steamer neared Norwich, the ship's engineer heard a strange crackling sound form the hold. Most of the crew and passengers were still asleep. Engineer George Norton, along with another crewman, went into the hold to investigate, and found almost the entire port side ablaze. *"Nothing but scuttling the ship could have put out this second fire,"* Norton later testified. *"We were all almost blinded and suffocated with the heavy smudge and smoke caused by burning cotton."*

The crew worked diligently to control the flames with pumps, hoses and buckets, but they were fighting a losing battle. Seeing that the situation was hopeless, Captain Brown ordered his helmsman to attempt to beach her ashore, but smoke had driven everyone out of the boiler-room. Without steam, the CITY OF NEW LONDON was at the whim of the wind and currents, and she remained in mid-stream. Flames were now engulfing the steamer, making it impossible to get into the storeroom where the life-preservers were kept. *"All hands to the lifeboats,"* ordered the captain, *"passengers first."* There was only one woman passenger aboard, and she was gently placed in a lifeboat first, but fire prevented the lowering of any other boats. Immediately the crew, with axes and crowbars, demolished cabins that weren't ablaze, to provide makeshift rafts for the remaining passengers and themselves. Roasting in the heat of the fire, crewman Matt Baker cut down doors and part of the pilothouse, making sure everyone aboard had something to hold on to once they hit the cold water. He forgot only one person—himself—and, with flames blistering his skin, he dove into the water. Without floatation, he soon drowned.

Captain Brown waited to leave his ship until all others had jumped overboard. He then leapt in himself, found a floating door to hold on to, and continued to circle his ship to help anyone who might be floundering in the water. Pilot Ed Ewen drifted to Walden Island on a plank of wood. Although half frozen himself, he swam back out to save others with his plank of wood as they floated by the island. He rescued three crewmen before collapsing with exhaustion. Farmers on shore, spying the great steamer aflame, rowed out to her, saving many who struggled in the icy river. Most of those who died—seventeen in all, only three of them passengers—were crushed, drowned, and burned by the very ship they had left in jumping overboard. The steamer, overcome by flames, shifted course by a change of wind and came rushing toward shore, barreling over scores of crewmen who were floating on the surface. Some dove underwater as the steamer attempted to run them down, but many couldn't get out of the way in time.

The only woman aboard, a Mrs. Adams, was saved. A hero's funeral was given to crewman Matt Baker at Norwich, and a benefit fund started for his orphaned six-year-old son. the captain and crewmen of the CITY OF NEW LONDON were praised by the jury of inquiry, by the press, and by surviving passengers. All that was left of the CITY OF NEW LONDON at riverside was a tangled mass of metal and a smokestack. Unlike her predecessor, the LEXINGTON, all aboard her had acted bravely at her demise. Under conditions similar to those experienced by the captain and crew of the "White Lady," the NEW LONDON captain and crew behaved gallantly, and all were considered heroes. Not one of them had acted cowardly, and one might wonder: why did all respond as cowards on one ship, and heroes on another? We might conclude that conditions at the time of disaster do not substantially contribute to the actions or reactions of the victims. Possibly heroic behavior stems from deep within the soul of an individual, or is the result of a collective spirit among the crew that determines their actions in times of crisis. If that is true, then the spirit aboard the ill-fated LA BOURGOGNE was extremely negative and bordered on demonic, for no ship that ever plied the North Atlantic has acquired such an evil reputation as did she, on the day of her doom.

There was a dense, smoky fog covering the surface waters some sixty miles off Nova Scotia that morning, and two ships were on a collision course: the 7,385–ton LA BOURGOGNE steamer, carrying 725 souls, and the three-masted bark CROMARTYSHIRE. It was 5:30 a.m., July 4, 1898. Captain Henderson, commander of the British bark, later reported that, *"our foghorn was being kept going regularly every minute. At that time I heard a steamer's whistle on our port beam, which seemed to be nearing fast. We blew our horn and were answered by a steamer's whistle, when all of a sudden she loomed through the fog on our port bow and crashed into us going at terrific speed..."*

Up until that moment, the French passenger liner was reputed to be the fastest, most comfortable vessel afloat, with excellent service and a cordial, experienced captain and crew. Within minutes, her reputation was tarnished forever and she became a nightmare— *"a ship of horrors with a crew of monsters,"* said one surviving passenger, and the name LA BOURGOGNE became infamous.

There was a booming crash and both ships trembled. The bark's jib-boom smashed into the bridge of the steamer, puncturing through metal to her engineroom. The two ships backed off, both with their bows battered in, and then they scraped each other from stem to stern, making a shrieking sound as they disengaged. In the LA BOURGOGNE engineroom, many of the coal-shoveling crew, called *"the black gang,"* were scalded to death by steam escaping from her ruptured boilers. No one was injured aboard the CROMARTYSHIRE. *"However,"* reported her captain, *"our ship was floating on her collision bulkheads, even though our bow was completely cut off, and the plates twisted into every conceivable shape. The other ship disappeared in the fog..."*

Captain Deloncle, commander of the LA BOURGOGNE, realized immediately that his steamer was in great peril. He was a highly respected skipper, who had received the French gold medal for bravery for saving the ship NORMANDIE when she caught fire in the Atlantic. He ordered the lifeboats lowered; but, as one passenger, A.D. Lacasse from New Jersey, noted, *"an apathy seemed to grip the crew, as if paralyzed by the suddenness of the emergency."* The steamer began to list to starboard, where she had been struck by the bark. Many of the starboard lifeboats had been splintered or crushed, and the portside boats were hanging high in the davits, making them nearly impossible to lower and launch. Second Officer Delinge filled two boats with women and children and attempted to lower them into the icy sea, but both capsized, spilling the occupants, all of whom drowned. This incident seemed to be what panicked the crew and many passengers. Members of the crew hit passengers, both men and women alike, to be first aboard the remaining lifeboats. Some even wielded knives to drive passengers away from the boats. Four survivors testified that *"we saw women stabbed to death like sheep being slaughtered."*

August Purgi, one of two passengers on deck when the ships collided, most others being asleep in their cabins, reported that, *"as I passed one of the lifeboats, where many sailors were clustered, they were cursing and clawing like maniacs. When I passed by , they thought I and another passenger, Mister Julien, were trying to climb in the boat ahead of them. He was struck over the head with an oar, picked up by two of the crewmen, and heaved overboard. I also was deposited in the water, and swam for about half an hour. As my strength was leaving me, I saw a lifeboat floating a few feet away, but when I tried to climb into the boat, several crewmen seized me and threw me back into the water. I tried a second time and again they threw me back. At last I suc-*

ceeded in climbing aboard, and someone said, 'Let him be!' and they reluctant-ly let me stay in the boat..."

Another passenger, Chris Brunen, was unable to get into a lifeboat as it was being launched. *"I was unable to get into a boat,"* he said, *"because the sailors kept shoving me away. I saw one crewman clout a passenger over the head with a bar or iron and kill him. Men fought for positions in the boats like raving maniacs, women were forced back from the boats and trampled on by human beasts. These fiends stopped at nothing. In one boat was a party of forty women, but so great was the panic that not a hand was raised to assist in her launching...Knives were flourished in every direction and used with deadly effect. Women and children were driven back to an inevitable death at the point of weapons...The scene in the water was even worse. Many of the unfortunates who were struggling and attempting to drag themselves into the boats and on rafts were rudely pushed back to their watery grave...When I was swept into the ocean, I swam for two hours before I found a capsized lifeboat, which I clung to until another swimmer appeared. We managed to turn the boat over and found four men and three women drowned, wedged into the boat."*

French passenger Charles Liebra, returning home from New York with his two children, aged five and seven, found a place for them in a lifeboat that was being lowered from the listing steamer. He was unable to get into the boat with them, *"for sailors drove me off with oars."* As his sons were lowered, Liebra jumped into the sea. When he returned to the surface, he was in time to see the LA BOURGOGNE sink, the lifeboat with his sons in it still attached to the steamer as she went under. Devastated by his loss, he climbed aboard a raft, only to be clouted on the head and shoulder by crewmen and thrown back into the water. He dog-paddled for hours in the fog until rescued by boats from the CROMARTYSHIRE.

Like Liebra, Jon Archard managed to get his wife and two children seated in a lifeboat that was being launched, but as she hit the water the steamer's fun-nels broke off and fell, hitting the lifeboat. Archard watched as a chain attached to the funnel cut his wife in two and crushed his children. He, too, jumped into the sea, but there were so many bodies and so much wreckage that he could not find the corpses of his loved ones. He tried to climb aboard a raft, *"but sailors beat me and cursed at me. One of them was Engineer Laisne, and he cried at me 'Damn the passengers! Let them save themselves. We save ourselves first. If I had a gun I would shoot all the passengers.'"* Boats put out from the disabled CROMARTYSHIRE rescued Archard.

The LA BOURGOGNE sank within fifteen minutes. In thick fog, the three boats sent out from the CROMARTYSHIRE managed to rescue 106 people from the steamer, but only one of the two hundred women, and none of the fifty-nine children. The bark managed to limp into port at Nova Scotia, where survivors were treated. But when relatives, friends, and the press were informed that of those rescued, only 65 of the 505 passengers aboard the LA BOURGOGNE had survived, there was bedlam at the docks and attempts were made to maul the 41 crewmen who lived through the disaster.

"*It is no less than murder,*" shouted a Mr. Steel, whose sister had been aboard the steamer. <u>The New York Express</u> editor wrote, "*Never in all the tragedies of the deep which memory marshals before us has so utterly shameful and cowardly a climax been enacted as that on Monday morning off Sable Island, Nova Scotia.*" <u>The New York Times</u> called it "*the greatest sea tragedy of the century ...It was a French ship and only one woman was saved.*" Although Captain Deloncle, keeping with tradition, had bravely gone down with his ship, and Second Officer Delinge, also going down with the ship, was praised for his conduct in lowering lifeboats, the entire crew of the steamer LA BOURGOGNE were whitewashed as "*beastly cowards.*" Surely, there must have been a few brave and honorable men amongst them; but whether they lived or died, they, too, were considered in America, Canada, and Europe the most horrible creatures ever to sail the seven seas. The surviving officers and crew were hard-pressed to find employment whenever the name LA BOURGOGNE was mentioned, and no other sailors would ship out with a prior LA BOURGOGNE crew member aboard. Paul Faguet, general agent for the "French Line," tried to save the reputation of officers and crew of the LA BOURGOGNE with an open letter to the press, in which he stated that, "*It was only at the last minute when all efforts were of no avail and the steamer was about to disappear that the sailors, by order of their chiefs, jumped into the sea and thirty-five of the sixty were lost...Of the eighteen officers, only three saved themselves, and then they did not leave the ship until they had done their whole duty...I am quite sure that a grievous injustice has been done in accusing the ship's crew of inhuman behavior toward the passengers. If any atrocities have been committed they were the work of foreign sailors who were in steerage, and comprised a variety of nationalities, principally Italian...*"

Faguet's words fell on deaf ears, and he only further stirred the cauldron of hate and disgust with people and things concerning the LA BOURGOGNE. Just the mention of her name brought loathing and disgust around the world. She became the flagship of cursed vessels in the sunken fleet of the North Atlantic. And to add further credence to her cursedness, a woman who missed sailing on the LA BOURGOGNE with her daughter, "*by a whisker,*" was the only one ecstatic when hearing of the steamer's demise. She thanked her lucky stars for being so tardy. Later that same summer, Mrs. John Phelps Firing and her daughter, Bessie, of Glen Ridge, New Jersey, sailed for their delayed vacation in France and England, booking their return passage on the liner MOHEGAN in October. "*I won't miss the boat this time,*" she laughed as she and her daughter boarded, but they might as well have been aboard the LA BOURGOGNE after all, for the MOHEGAN wrecked on October 14, 1898, on the reefs at Lizard Head, England. 150 souls were lost, including Mrs. Firing and her daughter. One great difference, however, is that the MOHEGAN crew was highly praised for their heroic efforts in saving many from the surf and jagged rocks at Lizard Head.

Raw panic obviously absorbed the majority of the crew of the LA BOUR-GOGNE, and mass hysteria, coupled with the dire will to survive, pervaded their minds, turning them into monsters. The few heroes aboard the LA BOUR-GOGNE, like Second Officer Delinge, somehow rejected the influence of hysteria and maintained clear minds in their efforts to help others, without regard for themselves. This remarkable ability seems miraculous when we consider the mayhem and insanity surrounding them. There are two great, acclaimed heroes in the annals of North Atlantic history who have not only felt the horror of a vessel sinking beneath their feet, but overcame their own terror to react with courage—and it happened to them more than once.

A teen-aged Gloucester fisherman named Charlie Jordan joined the Yankee Army to fight the Rebels of the South. He was captured in 1863 and sent to Libby Prison with eighty of his mates for the remainder of the Civil War. When he was released, he was but a skeleton, and all eighty of his comrades had died from hunger, exposure, and disease. He returned home to Gloucester, Massachusetts, and according to him *"did nothing but eat for six months."* In 1867, he became a crewman aboard the schooner DAY. A few months later, sailing to Boston, the DAY foundered in a storm off Cape Cod, throwing Jordan, his captain, and six mates into the sea. He tried to save one of his mates in the ragging surf, but lost hold, and the man drowned. Jordan struggled against the undertow and swam to shore, exhausted. He lay in the sand for what seemed hours, then got to his feet and stumbled to a seaside cottage, where the occupants gave him food and shelter. Next morning he received the news that he was the only survivor of the schooner DAY. Being an only survivor twice in his life, Jordan tempted fate again two years later by joining the crew of the fishing schooner HELEN ELIZA out of Rockport. Her commander was Captain Ed Millett, with an eleven-man crew, and she sailed in tandem with the schooner YANKEE GIRL, also out of Rockport. Fishing off the coast of Maine on the foggy morning of September 8, 1869, the wind began to pick up and the two captains feared a gale was brewing, so they headed their ships into Portland. The gale quickly became a hurricane, and the YANKEE GIRL soon disappeared from view of the HELEN ELIZA, never to be seen again. Captain Millett was having difficulty controlling the wheel of his schooner, and he couldn't bring her into Portland Harbor. In Jordan's own words, *"The wind picked up until it blew a regular hurricane. Both anchors were let go, but the cables parted...There was no earthly hope for us now. There was a tremendous sea running, there was little doubt that the vessel would go ashore at Peak's Island and, in that event, the chances of being saved were slim indeed. Captain*

Millett stood at his post of duty at the helm, to the very last moment, and in all probability received his death-blow from the main boom...The vessel struck heavily, smashing in the bow, instantly killing five people who were with me. I immediately ran into the hold, when a tremendous sea knocked off the deck, and I was swept into the raging waters."

Jordan was a good swimmer, but he knew he couldn't make it to shore without floatation—anything to hold onto. An empty barrel came by and he rode it in. *"The waves were fearfully high,"* he later reported, *"and as I was borne along, I passed George Clark and Ben Lurvey, two of my shipmates, who were clinging to a plank. I heard them both speak of their fearful position, and doubting whether they should be able to hold on. The undertow was very powerful, and the waves were heaving me toward the ledge. But, by the help of my barrel I succeeded, and inserting my fingers in the crevices of the rocks, I commenced the toilsome passage up the jagged sides, reaching the top completely exhausted. While resting, I heard the voice of Clark. I answered the call, telling him where he was, and enjoining upon him to hold on and try to get up the ledge. I did not hear him again, and probably the two men were instantly swallowed up in the undertow."* Jordan saved himself, as he did before, by walking to the nearest house for aid; he was the only survivor of the HELEN ELIZA. Back home in Gloucester, he was considered a great hero, a three-time winner. Each time he had battled the elements and, where others had succumbed, he survived, but he refused to go to sea again. *"That,"* he said, *"would truly be tempting fate."* He became Gloucester's draw-bridge tender, and on the morning of April 21, 1873, while straining to see the name of a schooner coming into port, his foot slipped on the draw-bridge ladder, and he fell to his death. His luck had run out—the name of the ship Jordan was trying to identify was DASH II.

To realize the impact that tragedy at sea can have upon society, one has only to mention the name "TITANIC!" The actions and reactions of passengers, captain and crew aboard her, for a period of less than two hours, on April 15, 1912, will be remembered, debated and discussed well into the twenty-first century. Prior to that day, she was the most beautiful, luxurious, fastest, and largest vessel afloat—everyone wanted to sail on her, especially on her maiden voyage. She was eleven stories high, a sixth of a mile long, weighed some fifty thousand tons, and could steam at twenty-five knots per hour. She was considered *"unsinkable,"* a God-defying term that her owners would regret less than a year from her launching at Belfast, Ireland on May 31, 1911. It was on that same day that TITANIC's sister ship OLYMPIC was placed into service, and two weeks later set out for New York on her maiden voyage. The OLYMPIC was not only TITANIC's sister, but her twin, equal to her in size, beauty and speed, built by her side in the same shipyard, but launched some seven months earlier. Although not as dynamic and notorious as her sister, the OLYMPIC had a jaded history, and a near fatal collision on her maiden voyage might have warned the White Star Line owners that they had created two floating monsters. Ten months to the day before the TITANIC disaster, the OLYMPIC smashed into the British cruiser HAWKE, head to head, on a calm sunny day off Southampton. The captain of the OLYMPIC was none other than Edward Smith, who later commanded TITANIC. The HAWKE's bow was stove in, and the OLYMPIC destroyed her quarterdeck, plus ripping a thirty-foot hole in her starboard bow, forcing her back to England. The thousands of people aboard her were livid that their North Atlantic voyage was canceled, especially the thirty millionaires, who had paid over $4,000 per person for a one-way ticket to New York. When the TITANIC hit the iceberg off Newfoundland and sank within two and one-half hours, her sister ship had put out from Southampton, but returned to port when her captain learned of the tragedy. There, the OLYMPIC's firemen, trimmers and other crewmen left the ship, never to return, one engineer commenting to the press that, *the recent disaster is too much for our nerves...these are hoodoo ships.* In a thick fog, off the Massachusetts coast, the OLYMPIC struck and sank a Nantucket Lightship, killing her entire crew, on May 16, 1934. The grand luxury liner was immediately taken out of service and soon demolished, finally determined by her owners, like her sister, to be a jinxed ship.

The "Unsinkable" Molly Brown of Denver had sailed as a passenger on the OLYMPIC when Edward Smith commanded her, and she was on the TITANIC as well. *And in a lifeboat rowing for my life, before I knew it,* she said, *and peering down upon us in the boat, like a solicitous father, was the benign, resigned countenance, the venerable white hair and Chesterfieldian bearing of the beloved Captain Smith. He directed us to row to the light in the distance— all boats keeping together.* Molly was just one of the 705 passengers and crew who were saved from the sinking TITANIC, 1,635 having perished. Yet all but one or two of the survivors had nothing but praise for Captain Smith and his crew. Survivor Lawrence Beasley states that, *All this time there was no trace of any disorder; no panic or rush to the boats and no scenes of women sobbing hysterically...When it was realized that we might all be presently in the sea with nothing but our lifebelts to support us until we were picked up by passing steamers, it was extraordinary how calm everyone was and how completely self-controlled.*

Passenger James McGough reported that, *The collision occurred at twenty minutes to midnight...None, I believe, knew that the ship was about to sink. When I reached the upper deck and saw tons of ice piled upon our crushed bow, the full realization came to me...Huge icebergs surrounded us. In lowering the lifeboats filled with women and children, and men as rowers, of which I was one, the blocks often jammed, tilting the boats at varying angles before they reached the water...We rowed to three-fourths of a mile away, to see the great ship go down. The ship's bands were playing, and their music did much to quell any panic...First she listed to the starboard, then she settled slowly but steadily. She was all aglow with lights as if for a function...and without plunging or rocking the great ship disappeared from the surface of the sea."* Some who went down with her were pushed to great depths, sucked down by the whirlpools, only to pop back to the surface, cling to wreckage and be rescued by other survivors in lifeboats from the 32-degree water. One was crewman Frank Tower who, when he came to the surface after going down with the TITANIC, saved a mate who had also been sucked down and spit out by the suction and whipping force of the whirlpool. He dragged John Cooper to an overturned lifeboat and climbed aboard, hauling Cooper up with him. They both were rescued within the hour.

Another crewman, Fireman Harry Senior, also managed to cling to an overturned lifeboat and was rescued. He reported, *"I saw Captain Smith jump into the sea from the promenade deck before the liner went down, with a little girl clutched in his arms. It took only a few strokes to bring him to the upturned boat, where a dozen hands were stretched out to take the child from his arms. The captain clung there for a moment, slid off again and swam back to the TITANIC."* Senior's testimony was just one of five that confirmed this heroic deed of Captain Smith. Others thought he committed suicide with a pistol as the ship went under. There was also a rumor that Smith had survived the sinking, and was living in Baltimore, Maryland, incognito. An old friend of the captain's, Peter Pryal, reported in the <u>Jarrow Guardian</u> in July of 1912 that he met Captain Smith on the street and spoke with him, then watched him board a train to Washington. Courageous or not, dead or alive, Captain Smith was blamed, along with the White Star Line owners, for the great tragedy. Before the TITANIC bumped into the iceberg, he had been warned, via his wireless operator, that commanders of six other ships in the area reported seeing great masses of icebergs in the shipping lanes. Also, he was speeding, obviously trying to make record time to New York. The owners were reprimanded at the court inquiry for not supplying enough lifeboats—there were only twenty boats and rafts aboard TITANIC, capable of carrying about 1,100 people, and there had been 2,340 people aboard her on this maiden voyage. Some of the lifeboats intercepted by other ships were only half-full with survivors. Also, many more of the wealthy first-class passengers survived, who had paid $4,400 per ticket versus the $40 steerage-class ticket, mainly because lifeboats were made more available to first-class passengers. With these major complaints, there were but one or two regarding the officers and crew of the liner. They were disciplined, brave, and thought of the safety of passengers first. The vast majority of passengers, too, acted nobly, especially the band, who continued to play music from a slanting deck as the ship went under. The old adage, *"Women and Children First,"* held true aboard the TITANIC. There was, however, at least one example of cowardice. Bruce Ismay, managing director of the White Star Line, was aboard the TITANIC, but escaped the sinking in a lifeboat—some say he had disguised himself as a woman, wearing a shawl to cover his face. Whether disguised or not, he still boarded the lifeboat designated for women and children, and he was severely criticized by the public and press. He lived the rest of his life in ridicule, and probably wished he had gone down with the ship, like Captain Smith, whom he deemed responsible for hitting the iceberg while running at full speed. Ismay's "unsinkable" liner, all 886–feet of her, now lies broken in two at a depth of over 13,000 feet, some 560 miles off the coast of Canada's Newfoundland. Underwater explorers have visited her tomb with underwater cameras in midget submarines, and have found the gash in her side, caused by the iceberg.

Two years after the TITANIC sank, in May of 1914, there was another great ship tragedy, considered the second most disastrous in peacetime history. The EMPRESS OF IRELAND, carrying 1,477 passengers and crew, collided in heavy fog with the coal collier STORSTAD near Anticosti Island in the Saint Lawrence River. The 14,191–ton luxury steamer sank immediately. She was only eight hours out of Quebec, heading for England. Just before the EMPRESS sank, she heeled over, trapping sleeping passengers in their cabins. One was Doctor J. Grant, who was thrown from his bed in the collision, but then found he couldn't open his cabin door. The ship was now on her side, and other passengers were walking along the outer hull. The doctor shouted for help and was pulled through a porthole to safety. Once free, he helped rescue many of the others who were trapped in the ship or floundering in the black waters. In the engine room, the crewmen had only four minutes to scramble up the ladders to the main deck. Steam pipes were bursting and salt water was quickly flooding the hold. Most of those working below didn't make it, but two who survived and helped others struggling in the water were Fireman Bill Clarke and oiler Frank Tower. Both had also been aboard and survived the TITANIC sinking. In a later interview, Clarke said, *"the two disasters were very different. The TITANIC went down like a little baby going to sleep, but the EMPRESS OF IRELAND, much as I hate to admit it, rolled over like a hog in a ditch."* The slim, black-faced Frank Tower said that, *"my pals back in Liverpool nicknamed me 'Lucky' after the TITANIC escape. I wonder what they'll call me now?"* Only 450 others survived the EMPRESS sinking; 1,025 didn't.

"Lucky" Tower debated whether he should return to sea duty again after two close calls within two years, but troubles were brewing in Europe, and he felt he should do his part for his country. So, after a short rest, he joined the crew of another large steamer. Surely, he thought, his troubled days of being involved in the world's two greatest sea disasters were over. The name of Lucky Tower's new ship was LUSITANIA. She was torpedoed by German U-

Boat 20 off Kinsale, Ireland, on May 7, 1915, and sank within twenty minutes. Only six of her forty-eight lifeboats were launched, and aside from a little mackerel boat, not one other ship was in sight of the sinking. That fishing boat and her six-man crew managed to pick up 160 survivors, which almost swamped their little sailboat, and she towed another lifeboat with fifty people in it into Kinsale. Some 1, 198 lives were lost, many American, and it was the crowning blow that brought the United States into World War I against Germany. Many believe today that the torpedo that sank the LUSITANIA was really *"the torpedo that ultimately sank Germany."* Like the TITANIC and EMPRESS OF IRELAND tragedies, the crew aboard the LUSITANIA acted bravely, as did her passengers. And yes, our hero Lucky Tower once again survived, and was applauded for saving two passengers as they floundered in the water. Even with a war on, however, Frank Tower could not get another job as a merchant mariner, for no one else dare ship out with him. He was a hero, and obviously very lucky—some even called him blessed—but other sailors feared to be with him at sea. He had become a jinx, a Jonah, and he was forced to spend the rest of his life on dry land. So, as the cowardly acts of men in distress at sea have, I'm sure, haunted them for the rest of their natural lives, self-preservation and heroics haunted the remarkable Frank "Lucky" Tower.

There has never been anything comparable to the triple tragedies of the early 20th century: the TITANIC (top) in 1912, with a loss of 1,635 lives; the EMPRESS OF IRELAND (middle) in 1914, with a loss of 1,025 lives; and the LUSITANIA, in 1915, with 1,198 lives lost (bottom). Strange as it seems, one man lived through two of these sinkings, and Lucky Tower survived all three.

The cursed steamer CENTRAL AMERICA, sank in 1857, with 444 persons losing their lives.

Sketch of steamboat GENERAL SLOCUM out of New York, heading for Hell's Gate, caught fire on the morning of June 15, 1904, and 1,003 lost their lives, mostly children.

X
THE DEVIL'S DISHFUL

If the Devil is active anywhere in the world, he is at sea. Sailors, especially in the earlier centuries, were well aware of this, and there are many seamen today who believe he is ever-present on the high seas, lurking behind each wave, ready to pounce on vessels and unsuspecting crews to work his evil ways. Landlubbers usually consider a seaman's fear of a water Satan merely quaint superstition, and the stories of Jonahs, jinxed ships and cursed vessels the workings of overactive imaginations. Sailors, more than any other working group, often carry on their person talismans or charms, in the form of necklaces, bracelets, tattoos, and other small items when they are at sea, mainly to ward off evil spirits. The fishermen of Gloucester, New Bedford and Provincetown, Massachusetts, are noted for carrying various charms with them to protect themselves and their vessels. Many of the old seaman's taboos are still in effect as well—no religious men, redheads, or women aboard ship. The original reason for keeping these potential Jonahs off vessels was because they upset the Devil, or so it was thought, and he would act unkindly toward the vessels that carried such undesirables. Having a redheaded woman on board was an especial affront to Satan, and many a crewman would leave his duties aboard if he saw that a redheaded woman was embarking on a voyage as a passenger with him. A young woman named Ellen O'Connor, a redhead from County Offley, Ireland, approached me in Dublin with the idea of writing a small book on the subject of "Strange Superstitions Of Ireland," and she told me that she had recently been refused entry onto the ferry-barge at Galway because she had red hair. The old ferrymaster considered her a Jonah. I thought the book idea was good, and she began writing while on a holiday in New York City. I was recently informed by a relative that Ellen never finished the book, however—while out sailing off New York, the boat she was aboard capsized and she drowned.

"There were three little freckle-faced redheaded girls sitting together, squeezed onto a bench at the stern of the steamboat," They, with some 1,000 other New York children, were going on a Sunday School cruise and picnic aboard the 250–foot, four-decked sidewheeler GENERAL SLOCUM. There were also some 200 adults aboard as chaperones. The steamboat, filled with frolicking children, left her New York City dock at 9:30 a.m. and headed for Hell's Gate on the morning of June 15, 1904. Off Harlem, Captain Van Schaick at the helm smelled smoke and asked a crewman to investigate. The crewman found the SLOCUM's cluttered storeroom ablaze, and initial attempts to put out the fire were in vain. Because of the giant oil tanks on the coast at Harlem, the captain decided he would try to beach the steamboat at North Brother Island, less than a mile away. Flames and smoke immediately engulfed the steamboat, causing the children to panic, and many were trampled in their

efforts to avoid the flames. In the hysteria, one of the ship's railings broke and many children tumbled into the sea; most, however, were being choked by black smoke, or burned by the fire. The crew manned the pumps in order to fight the flames with fire hoses, but the pumps were broken and the hoses fell apart in their hands. It was utter chaos aboard. Lifeboats were launched as quickly as possible, but they all sank on the spot—none of them were seaworthy. Children were screaming and screeching in terror and pain, and the adults seemed at a loss to do anything. Some jumped overboard, a child cradled in each arm. Most of them never made it to shore. The steamer soon became a furnace, and some jumped to the paddlewheel to escape the heat. A police yawl was on the scene within twenty minutes of sighting the burning ship from shore. *"I'll never forget the scene as we neared the SLOCUM,"* reported Officer Hugh Farrell aboard the yawl. *"Above us was a fiery furnace, and among those clinging to the paddlewheel was an old man, and on either shoulder was a child...It was hotter around that wreck than I ever believed possible."*

The blazing SLOCUM finally grounded on the island, and many children jumped overboard to make for land, but some of them drowned when they found the water surrounding the steamboat over their heads. There were over 200 children and adults clinging to the paddlewheel who were saved by the occupants of boats and tugs that came to the rescue. Eighteen year-old Charlie Schwatz swam back and forth between the burning ship and island twelve times to save 22 children and women, but he feared that the three shy, giggling redheads he had noticed as the steamboat left the dock were gone, for they had been sitting near where the fire had started. Nobody knows exactly how many lives were lost that morning, but the estimate was 1,033, the vast majority being children. One 15 year-old girl, Clara Hatman, was laid out in the morgue with the others, a tag on her toe identifying her. She had been pronounced dead hours earlier. An attendant saw her eyelashes flutter, and she was rushed to the hospital. She lived, but was the only miracle of the great GENERAL SLOCUM disaster. All else was horror and tragedy. The Devil had done his work well at Hell's Gate, and his dish was full.

If anyone dies with the Devil's curse on his breath, and that curse involves ships at sea, any seaman is bound to tell you that the curse is bound to become a reality. Such was the case on the west coast of America in 1857, when the steamer SONORA left San Francisco Bay, filled with passengers. They were mostly successful miners with their gold, heading back home in the East to spend the fortune they'd made in the Great Gold Rush. Among the passengers was Mrs. Henry Russell, newly married, but her husband was left on the dock. Helen Russell had her husband's gold with her, but she hadn't told him about her intentions to steam back to New York. When he discovered that she and the gold were gone, he rushed to the waterfront, but SONORA was heading out, although still within hailing distance. Henry Russell shouted, swore, jumped up and down, then tore off his clothes in frustration. *"You will never make New York,"* he cried hoarsely as dock workers laughed at his antics. *"The Devil will curse you and your ship, you whore,"* he shouted, and then he jumped off the pier and never returned to the surface. Helen had heard him shouting, but sailed on to Panama in the SONORA without incident. There, on September 2, 1857, she boarded the steamer CENTRAL AMERICA with Henry's gold, for her final lap of the journey to Cuba and then up the Atlantic coast to New York.

When the CENTRAL AMERICA left Cuba on September 8, there were 575 people aboard her, under command of Captain William Herndon, an experienced U.S. Naval officer. There was also an estimated two and a half million dollars worth of gold aboard. Off Cape Hatteras, in the midst of a storm, the steamer sprung a leak. Rising water in the hold reached the boiler, rendering the steam engine and pumps useless. Captain Herndon attempted to sail his ship, but the wind was too brisk, and a bucket brigade made up of all the men aboard could not keep up with the inrush of the sea. Within a few hours, the decks were awash. Two of the steamer's five lifeboats were quickly launched and immediately capsized, dumping out and drowning the occupants, mostly women passengers. In one of the boats was Helen Russell. It is not known if she had any of Henry's gold with her when she floundered in the raging sea, but if so, it only hastened to send her to the sea bottom. Henry's curse had become reality, and the CENTRAL AMERICA herself would soon go under.

On her slanting deck all was chaos, as miners who had spent years digging their gold out of mountains and streams agonized over whether they should try to save some of it from the sinking ship. Most disposed of their heavy money-belts. One emptied his carpetbag full of gold coins on deck and offered them freely to anyone aboard who wanted them—there were no takers. Those who tried to save their gold failed to save themselves. Most decided that their lives were more precious. The crew hacked away at the wheelhouse with axes to make a raft before the ship went under. Among them was Alex Grant, who had already survived three shipwrecks as a seaman—one was the previously mentioned steamer ARCTIC, sinking in 1854. Many clambered aboard the makeshift raft, but after eight days afloat, only three men remained, one of them being Grant. They were then sighted and picked up by the brig MARY, after they had drifted some 450 miles. Captain Herndon, after gong down with his ship, dressed in his formal uniform, was last seen by Alex Grant, *"standing ramrod straight,"* on a floating piece of the wheelhouse, *"and he was holding his telescope,"* but he floated away, never to be seen again.

"She gave a warning lurch before she went under," reported surviving passenger Arthur George, *"and then she plunged stern first, with every timber quivering. I heard no shrieks of terror, nothing but the rush and hiss or water that closed above her as she hurried, almost with the speed of an arrow, to her ocean bed. I was sucked down by the whirlpool caused by her swift descent, to*

a depth that was seemingly unfathomable, and into a darkness I never dreamed of. I then shot to the surface, and that was almost as painful in reaction as the pressure endured at the greatest depth. There revealed, rising and falling with the waves, was a sea of human heads...Finally I saw the lights of a rescue ship. She was the ELLEN. I never felt so thankful in my life..."

Mr. George was just one of the 131 fortunates picked up by passing ships; 444 others who had been aboard the CENTRAL AMERICA weren't so lucky, and they perished. The Norwegian bark ELLEN had altered course to rescue most of the sunken steamer's survivors, and when her captain was later interviewed and asked why he changed course in the midst of a storm, his answer shocked the public. *"A small bird had begun circling our ship,"* he replied in broken English. *"It would dive down and chirp over our heads, as if to tell us something, and then it would fly off Southwest. It would then return and continue its antics, and again fly swiftly off to the Southwest."* Being a superstitious skipper, he decided to follow the little anxious bird, *"and by so doing, I came upon the CENTRAL AMERICA survivors floating on wreckage."* Had the ELLEN not altered course, most would have drowned or died from cold and exhaustion. It seems that a flying angel in the form of a bird was as involved with the CENTRAL AMERICA as was the cursed Devil himself.

There was another Norwegian bark upon whose decks no angel dare tread. In fact, it was obvious to most that the Devil had stepped aboard her and made himself at home. She was the ill-fated SQUANDO. Like the CENTRAL AMERICA, her troubles began in San Francisco Bay, and ended in the North Atlantic, where she became a derelict. She came to the public's eye in the autumn of 1889, when the first mate of the SQUANDO was found dead in his bunk aboard ship. His cabin was splattered with blood, and he was without a head. The police seized the captain and his wife, and they were accused and later convicted of murder. The first mate and captain's wife had been feuding constantly, until she and her husband decided to shut the mate's mouth forever by cutting into it with an axe. Cleaned up and shipped out, the SQUANDO's second port-of-call was South America. A new crew didn't last long aboard her, and even though this second crew was not aware of her macabre history, they mutinied, killing the captain by cutting off his head. The owners moved the SQUANDO back to California, and a third captain and crew was hired, but within a month, on a voyage to the Caribbean, the captain died. A new captain was acquired in the West Indies, but sailing up America's East Coast, he too died, under suspicious circumstances. The crew sailed her in, tied her up at the pier in Bathurst, New Brunswick, and left the SQUANDO, refusing to ever sail aboard her again. The Norwegian owners considered their gruesome tales of shadowy figures roaming the cabins and strange voices that woke them from sleep as *"fictitious fairytales."*

The Norwegian consul of Canada was called in by the owners to protect the SQUANDO and her cargo at dockside, while they and their agents acquired yet another captain and crew. No seaman or captain in Canada would even think of boarding the SQUANDO, the owners were soon to discover, and the two watchmen hired by the consul to secure the vessel didn't last long on the job either. The two men, Haley Robinson and John LeClerc, had a frightening experience their first night aboard, as told later by LeClerc's son, George, who spoke of *"cold hands that touched them from behind and caught hold of their clothes, and they heard voices that told them to leave the ship."* George LeClerc also said that, *"items began flying around the cabin they were in, and a spike flew across the cabin and embedded itself between my father's feet. Robinson, looking out the porthole, saw a headless sailor on the quarterdeck. Bedclothes were pulled off them as they tried to sleep, and all lanterns aboard were snuffed out in a flash."* The two petrified watchmen quickly fled the SQUANDO. A week later, dock workers were hired to unload her cargo of assorted merchandise, but they lasted only a few minutes on board, running up the pier to dry land, shouting that poltergeists had tried to kill them by throwing handspikes into the bulkhead, closely missing their heads. No one ever boarded the SQUANDO again. She rotted away at dockside and sank—another victory for the Devil.

Six years later, as the gossip about the horror aboard the SQUANDO began to subside in the Maritimes, the Devil, in the guise of a crewman, boarded a Maine barkentine bound for Halifax. She was the HERBERT FULLER, which departed Boston on July 8, 1896, with twelve persons aboard. One was a woman, Mrs. Laura Nash, the captain's wife. Some of the crew were uneasy about having a woman aboard, and they related their feeling to First Mate Thomas Bram. He calmed their fears and reminded them that their voyage was a short one, and that Mrs. Nash had accompanied her husband on previous trips without incident. There was also one passenger aboard, Lester Monks, whom the crew assumed was a minister or religious man of some sort, for he constantly read the bible from the moment he boarded. Again Mate Bram assured the crew that Monks, despite his name, was not a man of the cloth. This superstitious crew, it seems, didn't want to incur the wrath of the Devil by allowing Jonahs aboard; little did they realize, however, that "Old Nick," as they called Satan, was rubbing shoulders with them. When the FULLER reached Halifax a few days later, three of her occupants were dead—murdered in their bunks, hacked to pieces with an axe. The victims were Captain Nash, his wife, and Second Mate August Bloomberg. Yet, of those remaining alive, only one knew who the murderer was. They were all taken to Halifax Jail and kept there until a lengthy investigation was conducted, but even after interviews, hearings, and a thorough search of the FULLER by Canadian police, they were still unsure of who had committed the triple murder.

It was during the "death-watch," as sailors call it, midnight to dawn, when the murders took place. Crewman Folke Wassen was at the helm. First Mate Bram was on watch, and all others were supposedly asleep. Lester Monks reported that he was wakened at about four a.m. by the frightened scream of a woman. Monks loaded a revolver he kept in his trunk and left his cabin to creep into the chartroom, where a lantern was lit. There he found Captain Nash on the floor with his head split open. Moving on to the captain's cabin, he found Mrs. Nash in her bunk, covered with blood. Monks then shouted to the men up on deck, *"Come below! The captain and his wife have been bludgeoned to death!"* Down the companionway ladder came Mate Bram, but seeing the gun in Monks' hand, he threw a belaying pin at him. *"This is mutiny,"* cried Bram, coming at Monks, but Monks hastily explained that the gun had been only for self defense. Bram then asked Monks for protection against the crew, and convinced the passenger that the crew had mutinied. They went up on deck together and hid there until dawn. With the sun to see by, they decided to go to the galley to wake the steward, Jonathan Spencer. Monks gave Spencer the gun and asked him to check the second mate's cabin, and there he found Second Mate Blomberg dead in his bunk, his head sliced open by an axe. Bram, who had told Monks he expected a mutiny, now called all hands on deck to tell them of the murders. Since he was now in command of the ship, he also called for an immediate funeral service to bury the bodies at sea. *"Don't throw the bodies overboard,"* said crewman Henry Slice, *"for they must be taken into port with us as evidence."* It was agreed, however, that they couldn't remain on board, so they were tied up in canvas and towed behind the FULLER in the ship's longboat. A religious service for the victims was held on deck with Bram officiating, but all were ill at ease, for they knew that amongst them was a murderer. The next day, two crewman reported seeing their mate Charlie Brown throwing a pair of bloody overalls overboard. When told, Bram had Brown put in chains. *"Brown's actions that night were suspicious,"* Bram wrote in the log, *"and he got himself all ready, as it were, to jump over the side, but he was guarded by all hands on board. At 1:30 a.m., he made an effort to rush to the bow of the ship, but was stopped by the steward at gunpoint."* Crewman Oscar Anderson then told Monks that Brown said he saw Mate Bram strike and kill Captain Nash, and that Brown was petrified that he would be the next of Bram's victims. Hearing this, Monks and Spencer seized Bram and handcuffed him. *"I am innocent!"* cried Bram, but when they reached Halifax, authorities didn't know who to believe. After two trials, it was Bram who was eventually found guilty of murder. It was disclosed at court that Bram had an obsession for wanting to skipper a ship, and previous crewmen under his command testified that he had once planned to kill the captain of a ship named WHITE-WINGS, but that there hadn't been enough evidence at that time to hold him for attempted murder. Most of the crew of the HERBERT FULLER, however, thought Charlie Brown was the murderer. Bram was given life imprisonment, but after fourteen years in jail, he was granted a pardon by President Woodrow Wilson. In 1919 he returned to the sea as a ship captain and prospered. He maintained that he was innocent of the FULLER murders till the day he died in 1950 at the age of 87. The barkentine FULLER, said to be haunted by the three victims of the axe massacre, was refused to be boarded by all seamen. The owner then secretly changed her name to MARGARET ROUSS and found an unsuspecting captain and crew in Florida. On a lumber run to Genoa, she was sunk by a German torpedo on April 27, 1917.

Did Charlie Brown really commit the murders? Most seamen thought so, for Charlie Brown was a redhead, and he was considered the real Jonah aboard the FULLER, not Mrs. Nash or Lester Monks. It was reported that Brown laughed hysterically when he was acquitted and Bram was found guilty. He left court and was never seen at sea or around the docks again.

Only 110 miles northeast from Halifax, as the crow flies, a discovery even more shocking to the people of the Maritimes than the FULLER massacre was made by a Captain Cunningham at Guysboro County Harbor, in May of 1844. It seemed at first to be a ship in distress, foundering on the rocks, but upon further examination Captain Cunningham came upon a sickening sight—there were but six of the original fourteen crewmen aboard, and they were all so intoxicated they couldn't stand or speak coherently. Empty bottles were strewn on the deck and in the cabins, and there were bloodstains everywhere. The name of the distressed bark was SALADIN, and Cunningham knew her skipper, a fellow Nova Scotian named Sandy MacKenzie. MacKenzie was nowhere to be found, but a large chest of money was found by Captain Cunningham in the captain's cabin. Cunningham felt that the SALADIN, though certainly in trouble, would not sink, so he placed some of his crew aboard her and sailed his ship into port for help. When the drunk sailors were retrieved from the 460–ton bark, the SALADIN and her cargo was salvaged and the six crewmen were jailed for mutiny and murder. At first they all testified that Captain MacKenzie had died of natural causes, and because of the smell of his corpse, they had been forced to bury him at sea, and that the other missing crewmen fell overboard in a storm. What they failed to mention was that there were two passengers aboard—one was the Devil, and the other, his son.

Captain George Fielding and his 13 year-old son, George Jr., sailed from Liverpool to Peru in the ship VITULA, bent on making their fortune. They were smugglers, and in their attempt to export a shipment of guano, Captain Fielding was caught by the Peruvian authorities and jailed. His son helped him to escape, and by hiding on a British steamer they were able to make it to Valparaiso. There, the SALADIN was taking on cargo, and at the pleading of Fielding, the kindhearted Captain MacKenzie took them in and promised them free passage to England. The SALADIN headed into the North Atlantic in early February, 1844, and George Fielding soon discovered that she was carrying a rich cargo of copper, guano, thirteen bars of silver and a chest of silver coins. He conspired with his son to take over the ship, but he would need more manpower to do so. Choosing the most disgruntled of the crew members, he persuaded four of them to join in a mutiny. These men were George Jones, Charles Anderson, Jack Hazelton, and an ever-smiling wiry redhead named William Travascus, who used the alias Johnson. By late March, they had devised a plan for killing most of the others and taking over the ship. They would then bury the silver bars and money chest on some deserted island in Nova Scotia, sneak into the United States, and return for the money later.

They put their plan into effect on the night of April 12th. With one blow to the head with an axe, Jones killed First Mate Byrie as he lay in a hammock on deck. They then called the ship's carpenter on deck and hit him square in the forehead with a mallet. Although he was not yet dead, they threw the carpenter overboard. Apparently revived by the cold water, he began shouting for help, arousing all others who were asleep below. The quick-thinking Jones, not wanting the others to discover their plot, shouted *"Man overboard!"* Captain MacKenzie ordered the ship be turned around to pick up the carpenter, and it was then that crewman Anderson clubbed the old captain with a mallet, but instead of falling to the deck, he chased Anderson in an attempt to throttle him. Leader of the mob, George Fielding, stepped in and *"struck Captain MacKenzie several times with an axe."* The captain was still alive and gurgling when the mutineers heaved him into the sea. As each unassuming seaman came on deck, he was struck down by hammer, mallet or axe, and his body thrown overboard, until eight in all had been murdered. The steward and cook, Galloway and Carr, had somehow slept through the massacre in their bunks below deck. When they woke and came on deck, the killers explained the situation and said they wouldn't be harmed if they would join the mutineers. After much deliberation, they agreed to join the others. The problem they now faced was that they had killed all the navigators, and no one knew how to get back into shore. The captain had written down a course to Nova Scotia and they followed it as best they could. Fielding suggested that all weapons be thrown overboard, so that one greedy mutineer wouldn't ever be tempted to kill another. They all complied to their new commander's wishes, and guns, swords, knives, axes and hammers were tossed over the side. They then decided to celebrate by opening the captain's liquor cabinet and inspecting his money chest. In their drunkenness, Johnson—whom Fielding had promoted to First Mate—found a pair of pistols that their new captain had hidden in his seabag. Confronted, Fielding said he planned to shoot the steward and cook once they sighted land. The crew then decided to throw Fielding overboard. The instigator of the mutiny was bound and gagged and dropped over the side. Fielding's son tried to stop the crewmen, but after disposing of Fielding, the majority decided that the steward and cook throw George Jr. to the sharks. He pleaded but the new commander, William Trevascus "Johnson", the redhead, demanded that the reluctant Galloway and Carr do their duty. So the hapless teenager was heaved over the side, and the SALADIN sailed on to be caught on the rocks at Guysboro, Nova Scotia.

The trial was held at Halifax on July 20th. Galloway and Carr told the entire gruesome story in detail to judge and jury, and because they were forced into mutiny and the murder of George Fielding, Jr., they were found not guilty. The other four—Anderson, Jones, Hazelton, and Trevascus—were found guilty of murder, and were hanged at Execution Hill, Halifax, on July 30th. All of them were under 23 years of age, and all but Trevascus, alias Johnson, were contrite. Johnson faced the hangman, so the newspapers reported, *"with a sheepish grin on his face."* Judge James Uniache closed their trial by saying to them, *"It is said that a wicked man, who was unfortunately a passenger, seduced you from your obedience to the captain with whom you sailed, and plunged you into crimes of barbarity and atrocity, the contemplation of which the mind recoils from. Unfortunately, this agent of Hades was placed in your midst, but now you must make your peace with God."*

All but Johnson, it seems, made their peace, and although hundreds saw Johnson swing on a rope with the other three, it is believed by many that the strange, smiling, red-haired sailor returned sixteen years later; again, according to him, his shipmate was the Devil himself. The macabre story unfolded on March 21, 1860, when two oyster sloops accidentally bumped into each other in New York Bay, off Staten Island. The mishap occurred due to the erratic sailing of one of the sloops, the E.A. JOHNSON. One man was seen aboard her, but he behaved strangely, trying to hide himself from the occupants of the other sloops. The JOHNSON's bow was damaged, but when the oystermen hailed her, there was no reply from the man on deck, so they sailed on and reported the incident to the New York police. One hour after the incident, the police found the JOHNSON abandoned in the bay and towed her into port. When they boarded her they found spatterings of blood everywhere—on deck, on the sails, in the cabins and on the hatches. Every item below was either overturned or smashed. Further investigation revealed that the sloop was owned and operated by a Captain Burr of Islip, Long Island. Aboard her when she left her slip on the Sunday morning of March 18 were Captain Burr, two young brothers, Oliver and Smith Watts, plus a recently hired deckhand named William Johnson. The police went to the tenement house where Johnson lived, and although he wasn't there, two men living there told the police that Johnson had just come into a lot of money, and had told them he was going to Providence, Rhode Island, for a vacation. Two New York police investigators were hot on his trail, and in Providence they visited a restaurant where a man of Johnson's description had just finished gin and eggs with raw oysters. *"How could the man eat oysters,"* officer Burke asked his partner, *"after just slaugh-*

tering three men aboard an oysterboat?" They finally found their killer asleep in a nearby boarding house and arrested him. His pockets were full of money, obviously robbed from Captain Burr, and he had now taken on the alias of Albert Hicks. He told the policemen immediately that he had murdered Captain Burr and the Watts boys. *"Me and my mate the Devil did it,"* he said, smiling. *"It was easy, but Captain Burr was a powerful man and fought desperately. Finally, we dispatched him, and then took care of the squealing boys with an axe. They gave us little trouble. After leaving the bodies on deck for about an hour, we threw them overboard."* Thinking that possibly there was a conspirator, the police questioned Johnson further about *"the someone"* he said he was with and who had helped him with the murders. *"The Devil himself,"* he replied. *"He also was with me when we massacred those folks on the SALADIN back in forty-four. They thought they hanged me, but they didn't. It was the Devil who really killed the men aboard the SALADIN. They hanged the wrong men."*

The police were astonished, as was the public when the newspapers published the story of the capture and confession. *"New York Police Capture The Devil,"* one newspaper headlined. *"The Devil Made Him Do It!"* reported the <u>News of the World</u> on April 8. At New London, Connecticut, as the train from Providence pulled into the station with Johnson aboard in handcuffs, hundreds of locals, *"all wearing top hats,"* tried to seize him for immediate hanging, but the armed guards stopped the mob, threatening to shoot anyone who touched the killer until his trial. The trial, such as it was, lasted all of seven minutes. The sentence was *"death by hanging."* *"You tried that before,"* Johnson smirked. Was this man really the William Johnson from the SALADIN? He looked younger than the proper age, about 37, and although his hair was *"reddish,"* it was determined by the authorities that it couldn't be. There was no doubt that the SALADIN's William Johnson was executed at Halifax sixteen years earlier.

This Johnson, alias Hicks, was merely demented, the court authorities decided. An estimated crowd of 12,000 came to see him hang at his place of execution, Bedloe Island in New York Harbor, where the Statue of Liberty now stands. Before meeting the hangman, he requested a tour of the luxury liner GREAT EASTERN, which happened to be in port. *"A delay of a couple of hours won't matter much,"* he declared, and his final wish was granted. Sitting at dockside beside the gallows was the E.A. JOHNSON, filled with angry relatives of the victims, present to see justice done. Johnson seemed unruffled. His *"shipmate, the Devil, is still beside me,"* he said, and as for Captain Burr, *"the old man's grey hairs glistened in the moonlight, and his venerable presence might have touched any hearts but mine and the Devil's; the children locked in each others' arms; the young man and just budding woman, the fond wife and doting husband; all fell beneath my murderous hands, or were made the shriek-*

ing victims of my unholy passion first, and then slaughtered like cattle." He was dressed in white shirt, blue pants and a Kossuth hat, which was removed to put the rope around his neck. There came a momentary hush, and then the trap was sprung. If he had indeed escaped the gallows at Halifax, he was definitely dead on July 13, 1860. Many in fact remained at the island celebrating his death, some pulling at his legs to make sure the life had gone out of him, others hoping he would resurrect himself. The press claimed in his obituary that William Johnson, alias Hicks, *"was a real mystery man,"* but the real mystery is whether his cherished shipmate died with him, or is he still floating around on the high seas, dementing the minds of sailors?

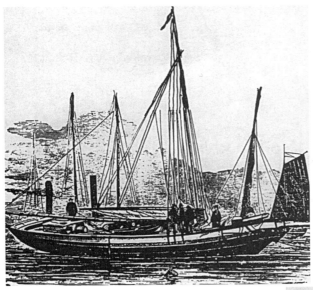

The oyster sloop E.A. JOHNSON and sketch of William Johnson, alias Albert Hicks, the multi-murderer, who claimed, "The Devil made me do it."

Bibliography

Berlitz, Charles. *The Bermuda Triangle*, Doubleday & Co., Garden City, New York, 1974.

Botkin, B.A. *A Treasury of New England Folklore*, American Legacy Press, New York, 1976.

Clark, William H. *Ships and Sailors*, L.C. Page & Co., Boston, 1938.

Colombo, John Robert. *Mysterious Canada*, Doubleday Canada Ltd., Toronto, 1988.

Creighton, Helen. *Bluenose Ghosts*, McGraw-Hill Ryerson, Ltd., Toronto, 1957.

Davie, Michael. *Titanic, The Death and Life of a Legend*, Henry Holt and Company, New York, 1988.

Fay, Charles Edey. *The Story of the Mary Celeste*, Dover Publications, Inc., New York, 1988.

Hoehling, A.A. & Mary. *The Last Voyage of the Lusitania*, Henry Holt & Co., New York, 1956.

Kemp, Peter. *Ships and the Sea*, Oxford University Press, New York, 1976.

Knight, David C. *Best True Ghost Stories of the 20th Century*, Simon and Schuster Books, Inc., New York, 1984.

Kusche, Lawrence David. *The Bermuda Triangle Mystery—Solved*, Harper & Row Publishers, Evanston, San Francisco, 1975.

Logan, Marshall. *The Tragic Story of the Empress of Ireland*, 1914.

Lord, Walter. *A Night to Remember,* Henry Holt & Co., New York, 1955.

Morison, Samuel Eliot. *The Battle of the Atlantic*, Little, Brown & Co., Boston, 1947.

O'Donnell, Elliot. *The Boy's Book of Sea Mysteries*, Dodd, Mead & Company, New York, 1972.

Snow, Edward R. *Secrets of the North Atlantic*, Dodd, Mead & Company, New York, 1950.

Snow, Edward R. *Mysterious Tales of the New England Coast*, Dodd, Mead & Company, New York, 1961.

Tisdale, Lt. Cdr. Mahlon, *Did the Cyclops Turn Turtle?*, U.S. Naval Institute Proceedings, Jan. 1920.

Verde, Thomas A. Maine *Ghosts and Legends*, Down East Books, Camden, Maine, 1989.

Watson, Julie V. *Ghost Stories and Legends of Prince Edward Island*, Hounslow Press, Willowdale, Ontario, 1989.

Whedbee, Charles H. *Legends of the Outer Bank*, John F. Blair Publishers, Winston-Salem, 1966.

Winocour, Jack. *The Story of the Titanic*, Dover Publications, New York, 1960.

Wisner, Bill. *Strange Stories and Legends*, New American Library, Signet Book, New York, 1981.